photographing Austin, San Antonio & the Texas Hill Country

Where to Find Perfect Shots and How to Take Them

Laurence Parent

THE COUNTRYMAN PRESS
WOODSTOCK, VERMONT

This book is dedicated to my wife and children.

Maps by Paul Woodward, © The Countryman Press
Book design and composition by S. E. Livingston

Photographing Austin, San Antonio & the Texas Hill Country
978-0-88150-941-0

Published by The Countryman Press,
P.O. Box 748, Woodstock, VT 05091

Distributed by W. W. Norton & Company, Inc.,
500 Fifth Avenue, New York, NY 10110

Printed in the United States of America

10 9 8 7 6 5 4 3 2 1

Title Page: Bluebonnets (**Lupinus texensis**)
close-up
Right: Mission Espada

Acknowledgments

Thanks go to Patricia Parent, Elizabeth Comer, Annette Pauling, Travis Wuest, Mike Burrell, Bob Daemmrich, Bill Sawyer, Louise Moore, Shalayne Mayfield, Mike and Debra Hobbs, Gerry Ingham, Ray Sierra, Keri Thomas LeBlanc, Amie Hufton, Lora Hufton, Lindsay Hernandez, Robin Harris, Jenny Lambright, and the staffs at the state parks, natural areas, and historic sites.

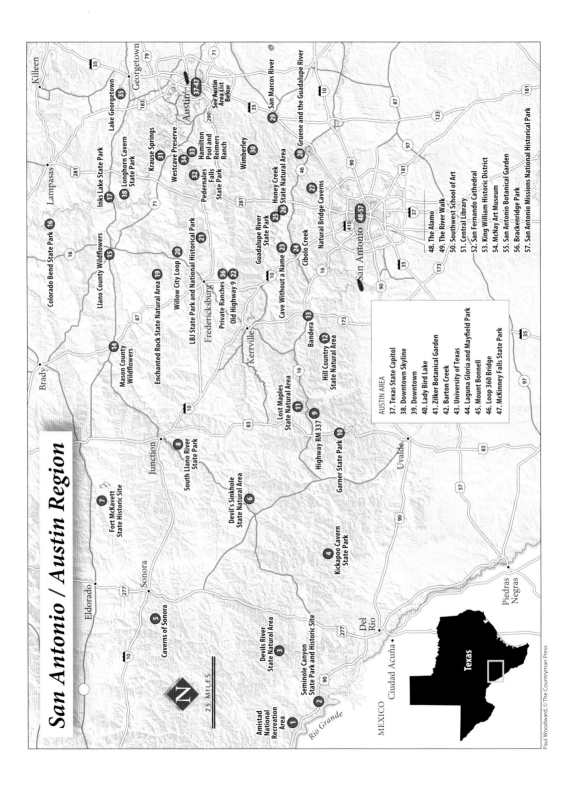

San Antonio / Austin Region

AUSTIN AREA
37. Texas State Capitol
38. Downtown Skyline
39. Downtown
40. Lady Bird Lake
41. Zilker Botanical Garden
42. Barton Creek
43. University of Texas
44. Laguna Gloria and Mayfield Park
45. Mount Bonnell
46. Loop 360 Bridge
47. McKinney Falls State Park

48. The Alamo
49. The River Walk
50. Southwest School of Art
51. Central Library
52. San Fernando Cathedral
53. King William Historic District
54. McNay Art Museum
55. San Antonio Botanical Garden
56. Brackenridge Park
57. San Antonio Missions National Historical Park

Amistad National Recreation Area
Seminole Canyon State Park and Historic Site
Devils River State Natural Area
Kickapoo Cavern State Park
Caverns of Sonora
Devil's Sinkhole State Natural Area
Fort McKavett State Historic Site
South Llano River State Park
Highway RM 337
Garner State Park
Lost Maples State Natural Area
Hill Country State Natural Area
Bandera
Mason County Wildflowers
Llano County Wildflowers
Colorado Bend State Park
Inks Lake State Park
Longhorn Cavern State Park
Enchanted Rock State Natural Area
Willow City Loop
LBJ State Park and National Historical Park
Private Ranches
Old Highway 9
Cave Without a Name
Cibolo Creek
Honey Creek State Natural Area
Guadalupe River State Park
Natural Bridge Caverns
Gruene and the Guadalupe River
San Marcos River
Wimberley
Hamilton Pool and Reimers Ranch
Pedernales Falls State Park
Westcave Preserve
Krause Springs
See Austin Area List Below

N
2.5 MILES

Texas

Killeen
Georgetown
Lake Georgetown
Austin
Lampasas
Brady
Sonora
Eldorado
Junction
Kerrville
Fredericksburg
San Antonio
Uvalde
Del Rio
Ciudad Acuña
Piedras Negras
MEXICO
Rio Grande

Paul Woodward, © The Countryman Press

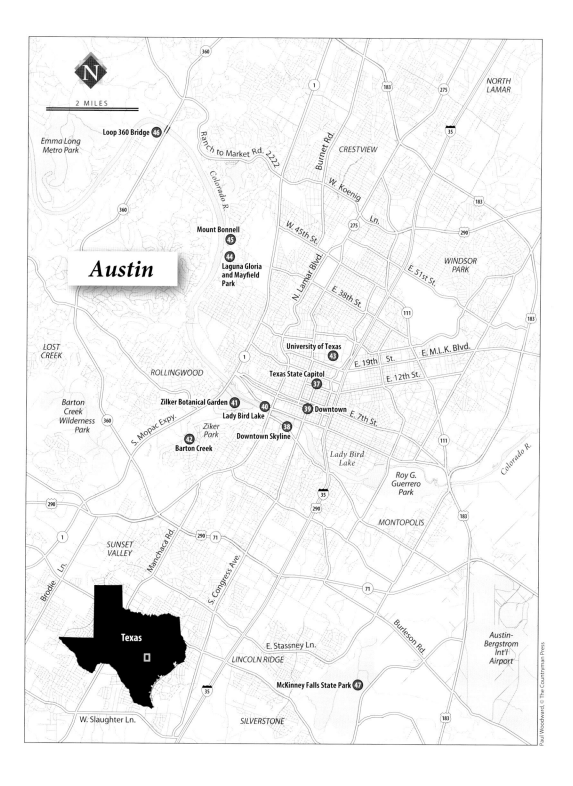

N

2 MILES

Loop 360 Bridge 46

Emma Long
Metro Park

360

Ranch to Market Rd. 2222

Colorado R.

360

Mount Bonnell 45

Laguna Gloria 44
and Mayfield
Park

Austin

LOST
CREEK

ROLLINGWOOD

Barton
Creek
Wilderness
Park

360

S. Mopac Expy.

Ziker
Park

Barton Creek 42

Zilker Botanical Garden 41

Lady Bird Lake 40

Downtown Skyline 38

University of Texas 43

Texas State Capitol 37

Downtown 39

E. 7th St.

Lady Bird
Lake

Roy G.
Guerrero
Park

Colorado R.

35

290

1

SUNSET
VALLEY

Brodie Ln.

Manchaca Rd.

290

71

S. Congress Ave.

MONTOPOLIS

183

71

Burleson Rd.

Austin-
Bergstrom
Int'l
Airport

Texas

E. Stassney Ln.

LINCOLN RIDGE

35

McKinney Falls State Park 47

W. Slaughter Ln.

SILVERSTONE

183

360

1

183

275

NORTH
LAMAR

35

Burnet Rd.

CRESTVIEW

W. Koenig

W. 45th St.

275

Ln.

183

290

E. 51st St.

WINDSOR
PARK

N. Lamar Blvd.

E. 38th St.

111

183

E. 19th St.

E. M.L.K. Blvd.

E. 12th St.

111

35

290

183

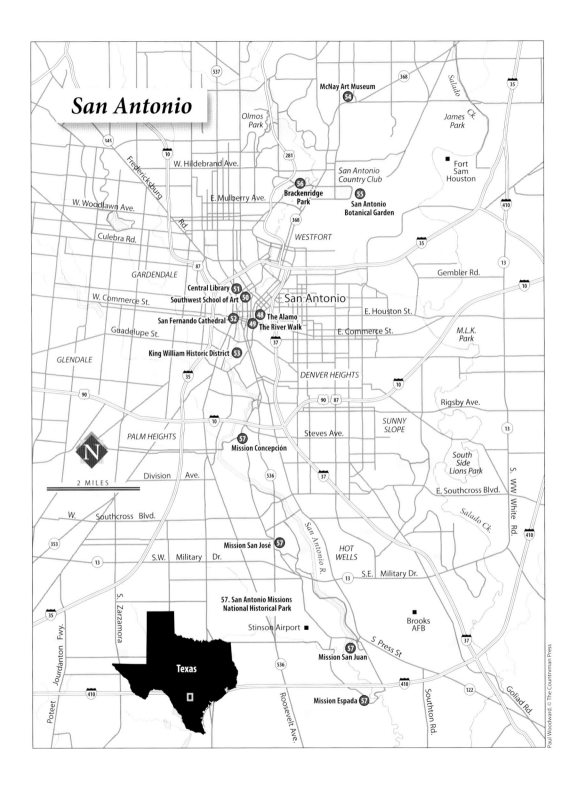

San Antonio

537

McNay Art Museum 54

368

35

Olmos Park

Salado Ck.

James Park

345

10

■ Fort Sam Houston

W. Hildebrand Ave.

281

San Antonio Country Club

410

W. Woodlawn Ave.

56 Brackenridge Park

E. Mulberry Ave.

55 San Antonio Botanical Garden

368

Culebra Rd.

Rd.

Fredericksburg

WESTFORT

35

13

87

10

GARDENDALE

Gembler Rd.

W. Commerce St.

Central Library 51
Southwest School of Art 50

San Antonio

E. Houston St.

M.L.K. Park

San Fernando Cathedral 52

48 The Alamo
49 The River Walk

E. Commerce St.

Guadelupe St.

37

GLENDALE

King William Historic District 53

35

DENVER HEIGHTS

10

90

Rigsby Ave.

90 87

N

PALM HEIGHTS

57 Mission Concepción

Steves Ave.

SUNNY SLOPE

13

2 MILES

Division Ave.

536

37

South Side Lions Park

E. Southcross Blvd.

Salado Ck.

S. W W White Rd.

W. Southcross Blvd.

410

353

Mission San José 57

13

S.W. Military Dr.

San Antonio R.

HOT WELLS

13 S.E. Military Dr.

35

S. Zarzamora

Jourdanton Fwy.

57. San Antonio Missions National Historical Park

Stinson Airport ■

■ Brooks AFB

37

Texas

536

57 Mission San Juan

S Press St

122

Poteet

410

Roosevelt Ave.

57 Mission Espada

410

Southton Rd.

Goliad Rd.

Paul Woodward. © The Countryman Press

Contents

South Llano River at sunrise with reflections, South Llano River State Park

Introduction

The Hill Country is the favorite region of Texas for most Texans. People from out of state who have never been to Texas often think of the state as being dusty, flat, and treeless, with lots of oil wells. While parts of the state do fit that description, the Hill Country surprises new visitors with its rolling hills, deep canyons, and crystal-clear streams, springs, and rivers. Twisted live oaks, junipers, cedar elms, and many other tree species wood much of the rocky country.

The Hill Country formed millions of years ago when a large limestone plateau was pushed upward along faults above the surrounding terrain. In the middle lie igneous intrusions of granite and gneiss. Over time, erosion carved river valleys and canyons into the Edwards Plateau as water ran off the higher country.

The ancient geology created terrain that holds great attraction for photographers. Today the rivers and creeks that cut into the plateau are lined with tall, bald cypress trees. Granite domes and boulders poke up out of the hills in the central part of the Hill Country. Historic forts and Spanish missions offer human subject matter.

Two major cities, Austin and San Antonio, lie on the eastern edge of the plateau along the Balcones Fault and yield distinctive photographic subjects. San Antonio has its famed River Walk, the Alamo, and historic Spanish missions. Austin has Lady Bird Lake, an impressive downtown skyline, and the beautiful state capitol building.

Central Texas offers something for every photographer: beautiful natural landscapes, old ranches, modern skyscrapers, historic buildings. This book highlights the best places to photograph in this part of the state.

Using This Book

This guide is divided into four main sections, the western Hill Country, the eastern Hill Country, Austin, and San Antonio. The individual entries give information on specific locations and the best seasons and times of day in which to photograph these sites.

Gray fox

Most land in the Hill Country and the rest of the state is privately owned. Texans are very protective of private property, so please don't trespass. Texans are also very friendly, however, and if you make an effort to track down landowners and express an interest in photographing on their property, they will often grant you access. I have been invited onto private property to shoot wildflowers when an owner driving by saw me shooting near his fence.

A good highway map is enough to locate most of the major Hill Country sites such as state parks. A Texas map book, such as the *Texas Atlas & Gazetteer,* from DeLorme, is useful for following back roads in search of spring wildflowers. The Gazetteer also has decent maps of Austin and San Antonio. A GPS unit is also helpful for finding your way around.

The Hill Country, while consisting primarily of private land, is blessed with a number of state parks that offer access to many of the most scenic places. If you plan to photograph extensively in the area, I highly recommend you purchase an annual state parks pass (visit the Web site of the Texas Parks and Wildlife Department for more information: www.tpwd.state.tx.us/spdest). It will save you money, plus support one of the state's best agencies. Other excellent photo spots are found in county and city parks and even along highway rights-of-way. The sites included in this guide are what I consider the best places to photograph in the Hill Country. At the end of the book you'll find a list of my personal favorites.

Mission San José, San Antonio Missions National Historical Park

How I Photograph Austin, San Antonio & the Hill Country

Prepare

Before you head down the road, do a little research. Read books like this one and get on the Internet to investigate state parks and other places. Acquire maps and/or a GPS unit. Allow time to scout locations, so that you can be at the right spot at the right time. Make sure your equipment is in good working order and that you have the proper filters and lenses. Clean your lenses and the digital sensor. If you shoot film, take plenty.

Some areas of the Hill Country are relatively remote, so be sure to pack sufficient water and food. Sunscreen and a hat are vital in a south-

Before dawn on the Guadalupe River in winter

ern state like Texas. Take insect repellent. Except after rains in the spring, mosquitoes don't tend to be bad in the Hill Country, but spraying your legs and pants will help prevent ticks from dining on you. In the western part of the Hill Country, check your gas tank regularly.

The photo locations discussed in this guide are generally accessible by passenger car and on foot, but there are some locations in which photographers will benefit from getting out on the water. Some of the best photo locations at Amistad National Recreation Area (Site 1), for example, are accessible only from the water. Check the individual location discussions for any special preparations that may be required.

Seasons and Weather

The Hill Country is made for spring shooting. Generally it's the rainiest time of year, turning the fields and woods a lush green and fostering abundant wildflowers. Creeks and rivers are running full. Lakes don't have ugly bathtub rings. It's my favorite time of year in Central Texas.

Fall is my second choice as a time to shoot. Summer temperatures have moderated and the sun has dropped to a lower position in the sky. While grasses will probably be brown, trees usually retain their leaves into November. Live oaks, one of the Hill Country's dominant trees, stay green year round except for a short period in early spring when they drop their leaves and simultaneously begin growing new ones.

Winter is a neglected season for shooting Central Texas. Much of the landscape is brown and gray, but the sun is low in the southern sky, allowing longer windows of good, slanting light for shooting in the morning and evening. Snow falls infrequently, but allows for beautiful, rare photos when it occurs. It's most common in the northwestern parts of the Hill Country. If you do venture out on snowy or icy roads, use great care. Secondary roads, espe-

Bald cypress in fall color along Cypress Creek in Wimberley

cially, may not be plowed or sanded, and Texans have little experience driving in such conditions. Another winter phenomenon also makes for good photos: in the crisp, chilly mornings after a strong cold front has blown through, mist sometimes forms over creeks, rivers, and lakes when the air is still. Golden light at dawn streaming through the mist makes for beautiful photos. Rain that falls as the front

A Hill Country ranch road at first light

pretty from the spring rains. Just work early and late in the day, when the sun is low in the sky. That's when the light is best anyway. By July, however, heat and lack of rain typically dry up the flowers and grasses. The sky tends to be hazy with humidity and the sun rises high in the sky, leading to flat, shadowless light.

Don't let bad weather keep you from shooting. Stormy skies are often the most dramatic for photos, but use care. Lightning is very dangerous, and floods, hail, and even tornadoes aren't uncommon in the area. Check weather forecasts and take along clothing appropriate to the expected conditions. I always have a plastic rain sleeve for my camera tucked away in my pack. I don't want the rain to stop me from shooting in great light.

The Light

Often the best light in which to photograph is right after sunrise and right before sunset. That may mean dragging yourself out of bed early in the morning or missing dinner in the evening, but that's when the light is happening. The shadows lengthen, giving depth to your photos, and the light is soft and golden. Plan to arrive at your destination at least 20 minutes before sunrise and stick around for 20 to 30 minutes after sunset so that you don't miss color in the sky. You don't want to be pulling up to your location at dawn just as the color fades.

Don't dismiss cloudy, rainy days. The soft, even light is ideal for wildflower close-ups, springs, waterfalls, fall color, and deep canyons; rain-wet flowers and foliage can almost glow with color. Just take care to keep your gear dry in such conditions.

The 10- or 15-minute period beginning about 20 minutes after sunset or before sunrise makes for great city and architecture photos. The city and building lights come on, but there is still a deep blue glow to the sky. Except for

blows through can improve the likelihood of mist by increasing the humidity. Be sure to be on location before the sun rises, as the mist burns off quickly.

Summer is probably the hardest time of year in which to shoot in the area. Sometime in late May, the temperature and humidity levels begin to climb into uncomfortable ranges. However, early summer is often still very green and when there is a really dramatic sky early or late in the day, dusk is my favorite time for shooting urban skylines.

Equipment

I typically take a professional full-frame sensor digital camera body and a backup body with 17–40mm, 24–105mm, and 70–200mm lenses. I also usually carry a 24mm tilt-shift lens to allow proper perspective when shooting buildings and to maximize depth of field for certain wide-angle photos. I don't photograph wildlife extensively; if you do, you'll want longer lenses. I also sometimes carry a 4x5 film camera with all its lenses, film holders, and other equipment.

I use a tripod for almost any kind of landscape or architectural photo. It's a nuisance to carry, but it helps guarantee sharpness and allows very small camera apertures for maximum depth of field. My main filters are polarizers and graduated neutral-density filters. Polarizers cut glare on foliage and other surfaces and darken the sky. Use care not to overdarken the sky, especially with wide-angle lenses. Graduated neutral-density filters help with high-contrast situations, such as a bright sky and dark foreground at sunset. The upper half of the filter will be one to three stops darker than the clear lower half to bring the difference in exposure between the sky and foreground down to a range that the camera sensor or film can handle.

I use a photo backpack with a hip belt to carry my camera gear. I sometimes hike long distances to get photos, so an over-the-shoulder bag would get uncomfortable quickly. I usually throw in a water bottle, snacks, a jacket, and a small LED headlamp.

Butterfly with basket flower (Centaurea americana)

Amistad National Recreation Area. Pecos River arm of Amistad Reservoir at the upper reaches of the lake.

I. The Western Hill Country

1. Amistad National Recreation Area

Amistad Reservoir is on the far-western edge of the Hill Country, where the green hills farther east fade into the Chihuahuan Desert. Most people drive through the area on US 90 or US 277/377. With the exception of the high bridge over the Pecos River arm of the lake, there is little to be seen from the highway to attract photographers. However, the lake hides some very scenic sites.

The lake was created in 1968 by a dam on the Rio Grande built for flood control, water storage, recreation, and power generation. The dam's location was chosen to be below the confluence of the Devils and Pecos Rivers. Lake levels fluctuate, with low levels being less favorable for photos. In early 2011, the lake levels were good. The lake lies on the border with Mexico.

Be sure to get some shots of the 273-foot Pecos High Bridge, the highest highway bridge in Texas, where US 90 crosses the lake west of Comstock. Take the side road to the boat ramp on the south side of the highway for a nice overlook on the canyon rim, or continue down to the water for a view of the bridge from below. The bridge is best shot early or late in the day.

Access to the best photo locations at Amistad requires a motorboat; distances are too great to reach via kayak or canoe. Trailer in your own boat or a friend's or, if you have the necessary experience, rent one from the outfitters on the south side of the lake along US 90. You can obtain a boating permit at Amistad headquarters, or from vending machines at the Pecos River, Diablo East, or Rough Canyon. Bring a friend along for safety and to serve as a possi-ble photo subject. If possible, have onboard a brightly colored kayak or other portable craft. Bring water shoes for wading. One word of caution: Be sure to stay on the American side of the lake if you do any boating here. Although Amistad hasn't had much problem with respect to criminal activity, the border areas of Mexico have become increasingly violent.

The boat ramp at the High Bridge will give you access to the most scenic part of the lake. As you motor upstream, you'll pass under the bridge. Watch for a rock shelter in the cliffs high above the lake on the right (best seen with binoculars). You'll be able to spot the large pictographs of the White Shaman Cave. The cave and surrounding land is owned by the Rock Art Foundation. Check the foundation's Web site (www.rockart.org) for public access times. The cave is reached via a trail that begins in the foundation preserve.

As you continue upstream, the canyon narrows and the walls tower above. Dead Man's Canyon forks off to the right and offers a good side trip before continuing up the Pecos. The large boulders that protrude from the water here can be great photo subjects, but they are also boating hazards. Proceed very slowly once you start seeing the boulders, and have someone at the front of the boat act as hazard spotter. The crystal-clear water, boulders, and towering walls make for beautiful shots, especially if the wind is calm and there are reflections. You will eventually reach the point where the Pecos River flows into the lake, halting further progress. If you have a kayak onboard, this area offers excellent boating shots. The best times to shoot here are early to mid-morning and mid- to late afternoon. When the sun is too low, no light gets into the canyon.

Make sure you allow sufficient time to boat back to the ramp or rental outfitter.

The canyon walls across from the boat ramp light up nicely early in the morning. A boat is not necessary for views of the canyon walls or the bridge from here. To photograph some good pictographs, boat downstream to the confluence of the Pecos and Rio Grande and go left, downstream on the Rio Grande. In about a mile you'll see a huge rock shelter, Parida Cave, with a boat dock where you can tie up. You can photograph the faded pictographs inside the cave and, with a very wide-angle lens, views out the cave mouth. Continue down the lake for several miles to the mouth of large Seminole Canyon. Panther Cave, a large shelter cave with a dock, has some really great pictographs. To get good views, walk up into the cave and shoot through the gaps in the protective fencing. Panther Cave is best photographed in the morning, before harsh sunlight enters the shelter.

The Devils River arm is the other scenic area of Amistad. From the Rough Canyon boat ramp (see directions below) head right, up the lake. Afternoon is the best time for photographs here. The canyon is not as deep and narrow as the Pecos, but still offers good photo opportunities. At the upper end of the lake, the pure waters of the Devils River pour in. Wade in and

Amistad National Recreation Area, Amistad Reservoir. Kayakers on the Pecos River arm of the lake in the narrow canyon where the river joins the lake.

walk upstream, getting shots of the clear blue-green water. Large fish swim around the deep holes. The banks are private property, so be sure to stay in the riverbed. On your way back, take photos of the towering, west-facing Indian Cliffs. The cliffs rise several hundred feet right out of the lake and catch the sun's last light.

Directions: Amistad National Recreation Area is just northwest of Del Rio, Texas. The Pecos High Bridge is a little more than 10 miles west of Comstock on US 90. For the Rough Canyon boat ramp, drive north on US 277/377 about 13 miles from its junction with US 90 and turn left on the signed access road. Follow it to its end at the lake. Seminole Canyon State Park has the closest campground for the Pecos. Extensive dining and lodging can be found in Del Rio and along the highway on the south side of the lake near Del Rio.

2. Seminole Canyon State Park and Historic Site

Seminole Canyon State Park is in the vicinity of Amistad National Recreation Area (Site 1) on the far western edge of Hill Country. The park is most notable for its desert terrain and impressive pictographs in Fate Bell Shelter, which can be accessed only via guided tours. Generally the tours run from Wednesday through Sunday at 10 am and 3 pm from September through May and once a day in summer at 10 am. Verify at www.tpwd.state.tx.us/spdest/findadest/parks/seminole_canyon/. The pictographs are in the back of a dim shelter cave; you'll need a tripod to get the best shots. Wide-angle to moderate telephoto lenses are best. The tour requires a short hike with quite a few steps down into and back out of a canyon.

The best sunset view in the park is at the overlook at the end of the Rio Grande River Trail (a map of the park is available online and

Fate Bell Shelter pictograph, Seminole Canyon State Park and Historic Site

at the park visitor center). It lies atop a high cliff overlooking Amistad Reservoir and can be quite pretty in good light and with a good sky. It requires a 6-mile-round-trip hike on a flat, easy trail, however, so do it in cooler times of year and carry a flashlight for walking back after sunset. Another good nearby subject for sunrise or sunset photos is the Pecos High Bridge (see Amistad National Recreation Area, Site 1).

Directions: The park is located along US 90 about 9 miles west of Comstock and about 41 miles west of Del Rio. It has a developed campground. Extensive dining and lodging options are in Del Rio and along the highway on the south side of the lake near Del Rio.

3. Devils River
State Natural Area

The Devils River has probably the cleanest river water in Texas. The clear, turquoise water makes an excellent photo subject. The park lies on the western edge of the Hill Country at the end of a long gravel road. The canyon bottoms contain oaks and springs like the wetter Hill Country farther east, but the uplands that dominate most of the park are mostly blanketed with Chihuahuan Desert vegetation.

Park headquarters and the bunkhouse are located along Dolan Creek, a big dry canyon that drains into the river. There is parking at the end of the open road. It's a 1.5-mile hike down to the river from here, following a marked road that is closed to motorized vehicles. Bring water shoes; the best shots will often be found out in the river. When there has been sufficient rain, José Maria Spring flows along the route, shaded with large live oaks. The park's river frontage runs upstream along the river from where the park road reaches the river. A high bluff rises abruptly above the river, creating a scenic backdrop for photos. For some of the best shots, walk upstream along the river below the cliff. Multiple large springs gush out of the base of the cliff straight into the river. Scattered boulders poking up out of the water make good photo subjects. The river offers a mix of deep swimming holes and shallows. Wade carefully out into shallow areas for good views of the river and cliffs above. Guard against stepping into a deep hole with your camera gear. A higher sun emphasizes the clear, colorful water. The west-facing cliff above catches evening light. After the sun leaves the cliff, consider staying for shots of the sunset sky reflected in the river if there are some clouds to the west. Or climb the bluff late in the day for photos that include the river in the landscape. Wide to normal lenses work best here.

Springs along Devils River, Devils River State Natural Area

Kickapoo Cavern, Kickapoo Cavern State Natural Area

Summers are very hot here, although the swimming holes in the river will offer relief. Carry an LED headlamp for shooting the sunset. You'll need it to on the walk back to your car.

Immediately downstream from the park's river frontage is Dolan Falls, the highest-volume waterfall in Texas. It's owned by the Nature Conservancy and is very photogenic. Check the Web site (www.nature.org/wherewework /northamerica/states/texas/preserves/) or call the Conservancy to see if it's possible to get access during a tour, as there is no access to the falls from the park. As of early 2011, the state had acquired a large tract downstream with 10 miles of beautiful river frontage. It will offer great photo opportunities when opened to the public.

If you stay at one of the natural area's primitive vehicle-accessible campsites, you'll need to bring water, food, and camping gear. Alternatively, you may rent rooms in the bunkhouse. Both require reservations two days or more in advance. Check the park's Web site for details: www.tpwd.state.tx.us/spdest/findadest/parks /devils_river/.

Directions: From Del Rio, go north on US 277 about 45 miles. Turn left (west) on gravel Dolan Creek Road and follow it about 22 miles to park headquarters. Be sure you have good tires and a spare. The park recommends a high-clearance vehicle, but I've driven the route before in a passenger car with no problem. If heavy rains threaten, don't make the trip. The gravel road has many low-water crossings that flood and wash out. Del Rio has the closest motels and restaurants.

4. Kickapoo Cavern State Park

Kickapoo lies on the dry western edge of the Hill Country. Its 6,368 acres offer hilly country dotted with Ashe junipers, live oaks, and pinyon pines, exclusive to this part of the Hill Country. The two main photo attractions are Kickapoo Cavern and Stuart Bat Cave. The park offers tours of primitive Kickapoo Cavern on Saturdays with advance reservations. There are no electric lights in the cave. You'll need a tripod and a portable flash or very bright flashlight or floodlight to get photos in the large chambers of the cave. During a time exposure you'll need to paint in light with your flash or other light to make the image. Focus carefully and use a fairly wide aperture and high ISO setting to reduce the amount of light you need. Check with the park to see what equipment they'll allow you to take on the tour (830-563-2342; www.tpwd.state.tx.us/spdest).

During the summer, Stuart Bat Cave harbors a large bat colony that exits every evening to feed. The thick swarm of bats often flies out in dense clouds, creating quite a photographic spectacle. The ridges above the campground offer decent views at sunrise and sunset with a good sky. Bird photographers can find the rare black-capped vireo here.

Directions: The park is located along RR 674, roughly halfway between Bracketville and Rocksprings. It has a small campground. Limited food and lodging can be found in Rocksprings and Bracketville.

5. Caverns of Sonora

Caverns of Sonora is one of the most beautiful caves in the world. The cave is privately owned, but surpasses most National Park caves in sheer concentrated beauty. Stalactites, stalagmites, helictites, popcorn, and other formations cover the ceiling, walls, and floor of some chambers. Water seeps through the cave, making the live, growing formations sparkle and shine.

The standard tour lasts about one hour and 45 minutes. With quick work and familiarity with your camera, you should be able to get some decent photos. Flash will help with subjects less than 15 feet away. However, photos taken with a flash tend to look harsh. If possible, take a flash cord so that you can move the flash off camera to get a side angle with the light for better depth. Visitors are not allowed to bring tripods or camera bags on regular

Stalactites and draperies in the Halo Lake Room, Caverns of Sonora

Caver at bottom of Devil's Sinkhole, Devil's Sinkhole State Natural Area

tours of the cave, so attach your flash to the camera and pick a zoom lens with a range from very wide to medium telephoto. On cold days, keep your camera warm and covered until you enter the cave or the lens will fog in the warm, humid cave air.

It costs extra and requires advance reservations (325-387-3105; www.cavernsofsonora .com), but the photography tours are far superior for obtaining good photos. Camera bags and tripods are allowed and groups are small. My preference for most photos is to use the existing cave lighting rather than flash. The cave is well lit by incandescent lights. By using high ISO settings and large apertures and by bracing yourself on handrails, you can often get good photos, especially if your camera and lenses have image stabilization and good noise-reduction capabilities. With a tripod on the photography tours, smaller apertures and lower ISO settings can be used for excellent results. Consider taking a bright incandescent flashlight with you on the photography tours. You can use it to fill in shadows that are too dark during long exposures. Although all of the tour is interesting, save your time and effort for the living, decorated parts of the cave, starting with the War Clubs and Valley of Ice.

Directions: From Sonora drive west on I-10 about 8 miles to the exit for RM 1989/Caverns of Sonora Road. Follow the signs south on RM 1989 for 6.5 miles to the cave. Sonora has plentiful food and lodging options.

6. Devil's Sinkhole State Natural Area

On a relatively flat hilltop dotted with live oaks and junipers, a vast gulf in the earth opens unexpectedly. The sinkhole forms an enormous pit from 140 to 350 feet deep. From a surface opening of about 40 by 60 feet in size, the chamber bells out into a huge floor area. When peering into the abyss from the viewing platform, you quickly realize that you are suspended in space from the overhanging roof of the chamber.

Although incredibly dramatic to view, the sinkhole is difficult to photograph from the surface. The best views are from the bottom

Fort McKavett State Historic Site. Commanding Officer's Quarters with ruins of Field Officers' Quarters in foreground.

looking up, ideally with someone standing in the bottom or hanging from a rope for scale. Unfortunately, unless you get special permission from the park and use ropes, you will not be able to descend to the bottom. However, there is an excellent consolation prize. In summer the cave harbors one to four million Brazilian free-tailed bats. They usually exit the cave for their nightly insect-hunting forays at sunset in a huge swirling mass that can be very interesting visually. The precise time of the bats' exit varies; ideally the exodus begins as the sun is setting, when there is more light in the sky, allowing faster shutter speeds to freeze the bats' motion. In addition, sometimes clouds will light up with color and offer a dramatic backdrop for their flight. The Devil's Sinkhole Society, a volunteer organization, offers evening bat-flight tours with advance reservations (830-683-2287; www.devilssinkhole.org) from May to mid-October, usually Wednesday through Sunday. The society also offers guided nature hikes and birding tours. Bird photographers may find Montezuma quail and the rare black-capped vireo, which live at the natural area.

Directions: All tours meet at the Rocksprings Visitor Center on Main Street/US 377 on the town square. The small town has limited lodging and restaurants.

7. Fort McKavett State Historic Site

The old frontier outpost of Fort McKavett was founded in 1852 and abandoned in 1883, but still stands isolated on a broad hilltop in the western reaches of the Hill Country. Many of the limestone-walled buildings have been restored to their original appearance, while some remain in ruins. Because the fort sits alone on a hilltop, with nothing blocking morning or evening light, photo opportunities abound.

Fort McKavett State Historic Site. Post Headquarters porch, with the parade ground and barracks ruins in the distance, in evening light.

Widely scattered live oaks add charm to the old buildings.

A variety of lenses, from very wide angle to telephoto, are useful at the fort. A tripod maximizes depth of field, keeps telephotos steady, and helps ensure that walls stay plumb and square in the frame. It will also aid you in shooting inside the restored buildings. Try everything from broad views with a porch in the foreground framing multiple buildings in the distance to zooming in on small architectural details. If you're lucky enough to get a dramatic sky, be sure to include it in your composition.

Shooting from late fall to early spring is best, primarily because the days are shorter and the shadows longer. In addition, the closest lodging options and restaurants are in the small towns of Junction and Menard, both quite a few miles away. Except for a few fast-food restaurants along I-10 in Junction, restaurants don't stay open late. To shoot at dusk, get to the fort by midafternoon. When you pay the entrance fee, ask if it's possible to stay on the grounds after the fort closes at 5 pm. Since the sun sets only a half hour or so later in winter, park staff are usually amenable to such requests. You'll need to park your car outside the gate and walk a short distance in once it closes. Two photo favorites are the headquarters building and the ruins of the commanding offi-

Reflections in South Llano River at first light

Directions: The fort lies about 23 miles west of Menard and about 40 miles northwest of Junction. It's well marked on maps. Food and lodging are in Junction and Menard.

8. South Llano River State Park

Because of its distance from large urban areas, South Llano River State Park is less visited than many parks, despite having a number of attractive features. It lies in a broad valley a few miles south of Junction, where the river snakes through the flood plain. An attractive developed campground in the park and nearby lodging in Junction make it a convenient place to get natural, uncrowded shots of the Hill Country.

The bottomland forest along the river consists of many acres of large pecans and other trees. Abstract images of large trunks and views looking straight up into the canopy are two possibilities. Mist can make the forest seem primeval. A 0.6-mile closed road leads from the walk-in camping area to a scenic overlook on a high bluff above the river valley that offers photo possibilities at sunrise and sunset.

The river flows with gentle rapids and flat reflecting pools. The water is clear, with a turquoise cast that shows up best when the sun is some distance above the horizon. Fall and spring generally offer the best shooting. In spring, beginning April 1 when the bottomland forest is open to the public, the vegetation is green and river levels are higher. In fall, still mornings after the first cold fronts can make for moody shots when mist hangs over the river at dawn. Cold winter mornings can also offer misty river shots, but the trees will be leafless then, creating a more stark look. In summer, the river is pretty, but the weather is hot and humid. However, it's the best time to photograph canoeists and tube riders floating on the river. The water is calm below the west river-

cer's quarters. If there are clouds in the sky, stay a bit past sunset. You may be able to get nice shots of the fort with a colorful sky. If you'd like to take sunrise shots, inquire the day before your visit to see if it's possible to gain entry before the fort opens at 8 am (325-396-2358, www.visitfortmckavett.com).

Especially in spring, consider walking down to Government Spring. Water gushes out of the ground in several places under a surprisingly lush canopy of pecan and other trees.

bank near the entrance, offering the potential for great reflections of the sunrise sky. Morning mist is a bonus.

The park's bottomland harbors hundreds of wild turkeys in winter, a boon to wildlife photographers. To protect the birds, the park closes the bottomland trails, but the turkeys can be photographed relatively easily from park roadsides and blinds with medium and long telephoto lenses. Be out at sunrise and sunset for the best opportunities.

Backlit hills and valleys off RM 337 at sunrise

Directions: South Llano River State Park is about 5 miles south of Junction along US 377. The park has camping, and Junction has plentiful motels and restaurants.

9. Highway RM 337

This highway is quite scenic, particularly the stretch between Medina and Leakey. The road traverses from east to west that part of the Hill Country most deserving of the name. The Ed-

Frio River with bald cypress trees in fall, Garner State Park

wards Plateau uplift was greatest on the southern edge. Rivers such as the Frio, Sabinal, Medina, and Nueces have cut deeply here, creating deep canyons and rugged hills.

This drive is best done early or late in the day. In fall and winter the grasses will be brown and gold. The sun will be lower in the sky, giving you a longer shooting window with long shadows and golden light. In spring and early summer, the hills and valleys will be lush and green. With a medium to long telephoto lens, you can create photos that show patterns of multiple hills receding into the distance from several places along the drive. The ridgetop to the west of Vanderpool offers great views at sunrise from the highway and a small rest area.

Several river crossings offer good views of cypress-lined Hill Country streams. Just west of Medina the road crosses one fork of the Medina River. The highway crosses the Sabinal just before Vanderpool and the Frio just before Leakey. The river crossings offer good photo sites not only on sunny days, but also on cloudy soft-light days. On cloudy days don't include much sky in your composition. It just goes white. The cypresses will be lush and green in spring and summer. In November, they will often have an attractive rusty color. On cold, still mornings, mist can sometimes hang over the rivers, giving your photos an ethereal look.

Directions: Texas RM 337 crosses the southern edge of the Hill Country between Medina and Camp Wood. The route passes through private land for the whole drive, so stay on the highway right-of-way. There is limited food and lodging in Medina, Vanderpool, Leakey, and Utopia.

10. Garner State Park

Garner State Park lies on the southern edge of the Hill Country, on the Frio River in an area of broad valleys and large hills. The clear, cypress-lined river offers many photo opportunities at all times of year. A small low-water dam creates a large pool in the river in the heart of the park.

Garner is one of the most popular parks in Texas, so avoid it on weekends unless you want to photograph people swimming, wading, and floating in the river. Any day of the week in summer is very busy, so I tend to limit my visits to other times of year. The best photo sites will be found along the river near the Pecan Grove and Oakmont campgrounds. Cypresses line the riverbank here below the towering bluff above. Trees and sky reflect in still areas of the river when the wind is calm. Walk along the bank and look for the perfect composition.

Sunrise, when early light hits the trees and river, is generally the best time to shoot. In late afternoon, the bluffs to the west shade the river just as the light starts to get good. In addition, early in the morning there will rarely be people on the banks or in the river. This is especially important in summer or on weekends. April and May, when the cypress trees have leafed out, is probably the best time of year for photos. In November the cypresses turn a rusty orange, offering another good time to shoot. Sometimes, at dawn after a strong cold front has passed through and the air has stilled, mist will hang over the river. Arrive before dawn; the sun will quickly burn the mist off. Try very wide shots, with the river or cypress trunks in the foreground. Or use a telephoto and selectively shoot just a bit of the river and an isolated cypress.

The high bluff above the river to the south of Pecan Grove Campground has rocky trails to the top. It offers great views of the surrounding area. As with the river, sunrise is the best time to be up there, although the light is good about an hour before sunset. It takes about 15 to 30 minutes to hike to the top.

Directions: Garner State Park is situated along US 83 about 10 miles south of Leakey. Pick up a map at the park entrance to locate the places discussed above. (Downloadable maps are also available on the park Web site, www.tpwd .state.tx.us/spdest/findadest/parks/garner.) The park has camping. The area around Concan and Leakey has scattered motels, cabins, bed & breakfast inns, and restaurants.

11. Lost Maples State Natural Area

Lost Maples State Natural Area is located in the most hilly section of the Hill Country. Because the canyons here are deep and narrow, they offer an environment more protected from the sun and wind than most of the Hill Country. These sheltered canyons harbor vegetation such as the bigtooth maple that isn't found elsewhere in Central Texas. About 11 miles of hiking trails take you up canyons, over ridges, and past many attractive trees. The maples turn orange and red in fall. Cherry trees often add a nice gold color.

Because fall color is rare in Texas, Lost Maples can be jammed during autumn weekends. Be sure to arrive at the park early in the morning. Once the parking lots fill up, the park limits vehicle entry. If possible come on a weekday. Color is best from late October through the middle of November. The park Web site provides regular updates on the fall foliage (www.tpwd.state.tx.us/spdest/findadest/parks /lost_maples/), as well as a map of the park. The color varies widely from year to year depending on rainfall, temperature, and wind. Some years it can be spectacular, other years bland.

For the best views of the maples, drive to the large parking lot at the end of the main park road. Some photo-worthy maples and cherries are along the Sabinal River bottom and on the

Bigtooth maples with fall color in the Sabinal River Canyon, Lost Maples State Natural Area

Fall leaves on wet limestone boulder, Lost Maples State Natural Area

feel energetic, follow the trail up out of Hale Hollow, over the ridge, and down to Can Creek. There are some maples around the pond at Can Creek and just downstream of the pond that make good photo subjects. To do the loop, follow the trail down Can Creek back to the main park road, photographing maples and the creek as you go. To enlarge the loop, follow Can Creek up to Mystic Canyon and take the West Trail all the way around and back to the trail below the pond.

Although fall color yields the best photos at Lost Maples, April can also be a good month to photograph in the area. The creeks and river usually have more water, the vegetation is lush and green, and the crowds are gone.

Unfortunately the area's maples are experiencing a slow decline. An overpopulation of deer in the Hill Country prevents most new maple seedlings from reaching maturity, and recent serious droughts and windstorms have taken their toll on existing trees.

Directions: Lost Maples State Natural Area is off RM 187 a few miles north of Vanderpool. The Vanderpool/Utopia area has quite a few cabins and bed & breakfast establishments. Utopia has a restaurant or two. If you plan to visit during fall-color season, reserve a park campsite or lodging well in advance.

12. Hill Country State Natural Area

Hill Country State Natural Area, although not far from San Antonio, is surprisingly lightly visited. With a large trail network spread over about 5,370 acres, it's popular with hikers, mountain bikers, and equestrians. It offers photographers a large swath of hilly terrain to shoot.

Like other areas along the southern edge of the Hill Country, the terrain here is quite steep and hilly. Pick up a trail map at park headquar-

north-facing slope just south of the parking lot. Try for some shots here with both fall color and water. From the end of the parking lot, take the Maple Trail up the canyon (it forks left almost immediately from the East Trail). It winds through a nice grove and then crosses the creek and rejoins the East Trail. Continue up the canyon on the wide, easy trail. Just past the primitive backpacking campsite, the maples increase in number again as the canyon narrows into Hale Hollow. There are great compositions here of the curving limestone canyon walls, small stream, and colorful foliage. If you ters when you arrive (also available online at www.tpwd.state.tx.us/spdest/findadest/parks /hill_country). The best areas for views are in the northwest quadrant of the park along some of the hiking trails. The hands-down best view-point for photos is along the Twin Peaks Trail, marked 5b on the trail map. The small loop fol-lows along the rim of one of the highest bluffs in the park and offers expansive, unobstructed views in almost all directions, particularly to the west and south. Bring a flashlight and stay until sunset, the best time for views here. As the light turns gold, the rocks on the rim make a good foreground to lead you into the broad vista be-yond. A dramatic sky is a bonus. Consider tak-ing a friend with you to stand on the rim and add scale to your shots. The hike is about 1.5 miles round trip with some climbing. Start at the parking area along the park road just north of the Trailhead Equestrian Camp Area.

Another good overlook is at the south end of Trail 4b, part of the Cougar Canyon Trail. It looks mostly south and southwest and requires a longer walk. For the best water shots of West Verde Creek, try for shots of some small cas-cades along the creek near the Chaquita Falls Camp Area. Comanche Bluff, above the camp area of the same name, also has some views, al-though not as impressive as the other two. Dawn is the best time to shoot here. Elsewhere in the park, consider climbing to high points for morning or evening light. Shoot wildflower

Waterfall, West Verde Creek, Hill Country State Natural Area

A hiker on the Twin Peaks overlook at last light, Hill Country State Natural Area

close-ups in the spring and grassy fields in the creek bottoms.

Directions: From Bandera, take TX 173 just across the Medina River and turn right on RM 1077. Follow it about 10 miles south to the end of pavement at the park entrance. Bring drinking water, as potable water is not available. The park offers primitive campsites, and Bandera has motels and restaurants.

13. Bandera

Bandera is a pretty Hill Country town on the banks of the Medina River. While some of the newer areas sprawling east toward San Antonio along TX 16 aren't particularly attractive, the center of town has some rustic charm with a western-cowboy feel. The attractive, historic courthouse along TX 16 just west of downtown makes a good photo subject. Try shooting broad shots with a wide-angle lens or, even better, a wide-angle tilt-shift lens to correct for perspective problems. Use a longer lens to zoom in on architectural details. Late afternoon to sunset gives the best results.

Just south of downtown by the TX 173 bridge is an attractive park on the Medina River. Most of the river here is still and calm, with deep, clear pools and reflections of the bald cypress trees that line its banks. The park stretches some distance upstream to where the river has some active flow. Walk along the bank and look for compositions. Try wide shots with cypress trunks in the foreground and telephoto shots that isolate a few trees and a bit of river. The opposite bank rises fairly quickly and is undeveloped, so even though you're photographing from mowed parkland on your side of the river, the photos will look natural. Late afternoon light and soft overcast light both work well. If you catch the river on a still, chilly dawn with mist rising, work fast: it's a beautiful but short-lived phenomenon. Spring and

Polly's Chapel, Bandera County

early summer when the trees are lush and green, and November, when the cypresses turn rust red, are the best times of year.

Consider following the river west along TX 16 toward Medina. The land along the way is private, but where the highway crosses the river, you can get some nice views of the cypress-lined waterway. Several side roads cross the river also, so scout them for good compositions. As with photographing the river in the park in Bandera, early and late in the day work best, along with cloudy days.

Another good site for photography is Polly's Chapel, named after its builder, Policarpo (Polly) Rodriguez, a Methodist preacher. To visit the structure, a Texas Historic Landmark, drive east of Bandera on TX 16 about 5 miles to the turnoff on the left for Privilege Creek Road. Follow the road north about 3 miles,

watching for the small chapel signs at two junctions. The road turns to gravel along the way. The last short segment is a bit rough, so drive slowly.

The small stone chapel, built in 1882 of native limestone, is hidden away in a grove of live oaks and junipers. There are no regular services, but it is used for weddings and other special events. Try to arrive before dawn for the best light. The chapel's entrance faces the rising sun. Some of the oaks cast dark shadows across the front, so shoot as soon as the sun hits, before the contrast gets too high and the light loses its warmth. Wide-angle and tilt-shift lenses are most useful. Watch that you don't get your own shadow in your photos.

Directions: Bandera lies in the Hill Country about 40 miles northwest of San Antonio. Food and lodging are plentiful.

Medina River in Bandera with bald cypress trees in fall

Mason County wildflowers: bluebonnets (Lupinus texensis), *Indian blanket* (Gaillardia pulchella), *and bitterweed* (Helenium amarum) *at sunset*

II. The Eastern Hill Country

14. Mason County Wildflowers

The small town of Mason lies in a part of the Hill Country known as the Llano Uplift. In this area large igneous intrusions and metamorphic rocks are exposed to the surface, unlike the limestones that blanket the rest of the Hill Country. These ancient rocks were exposed when the much younger sedimentary rocks eroded away. The most famous outcrop is Enchanted Rock (see Site 19). The soil created by erosion of these rocks is more fertile than that in the limestone areas of most of the Hill Country. Hence when the wildflowers bloom, these areas generally have the best displays.

The wildflowers vary widely from year to year. Dry years usually mean a poor showing of flowers everywhere. However, even in good years, the blooms can differ significantly from place to place. A place that had great flowers one year may not have a good display the following year even with adequate rains. Conversely, a spot that hasn't had good flowers for years may be blanketed with blooms. Usually the best strategy for finding flowers is to check with state parks in the area, such as Enchanted Rock or Inks Lake, and to search online for word of good places to look. Flowers such as bluebonnets and Indian paintbrush come out first, usually peaking in early to mid-April. If rains continue, the flowers continue to change species, usually becoming more yellow.

Wildflowers thrive along main highways in the Hill Country as well as on small county roads, where you won't have the obnoxious traffic whizzing past. The *Texas Atlas & Gazetteer* from DeLorme is a good resource to have on hand when setting out on a wildflower expedition. Try the loop of TX 29, FM 1900,

Mason County wildflowers: Indian blanket (Gaillardia pulchella), *bitterweed* (Helenium amarum), *phlox* (Phlox *sp.*)

FM 2618, and FM 386 on the northeast side of Mason. Nice fields of Indian blanket, phlox, lazy daisies, and bluebonnets grow along this loop, and on the little county roads that branch off it. Another route is to take TX 29 east toward Llano and then turn right on FM 2768 to the tiny village of Castell. The field by the little Trinity United Methodist Church in town can have a fabulous mix of flowers—bluebonnets, Indian paintbrush, Indian blanket, and other species. The church itself makes a nice subject, especially late in the day. From the west side of Castell, take the gravel county road that goes south to the village of Loyal Valley, which can be great for flowers.

Other subjects of interest in the area include the Mason County courthouse, an attractive building, if somewhat difficult to shoot. Try early and late in the day and concentrate on architectural details. A few miles south on US 87, from Loyal Valley to Cherry Spring, look for the lonely church steeple off in the distance to the east. The Christ Lutheran Church is on a paved county road just off 87. The front faces east and is best shot in the morning, although oaks will block light off some of it. Evening brings good, unobstructed light to the back and south side.

Continue to explore some of the other back roads in the area. Try FM 152 between US 87 and Castell and FM 783 south of US 87, along with the smaller county roads. You never know what wildflowers you'll find. If you leave your car, remember to stay by the road, even if there isn't a fence. This is all private land.

Directions: Mason is a small town in the northwestern part of the Hill Country, northwest of Fredericksburg, and has restaurants and several lodging options.

15. Llano County Wildflowers

Just like adjoining Mason County, described above, much of Llano County has nonlimestone soils that favor wildflowers. Before you head out to shoot them, get a few photos of the beautiful, historic courthouse in Llano. Early morning is probably the best time. Use tilt-shift and wide-angle lenses to get the entire courthouse in the frame, but consider a telephoto for details.

As discussed in the Mason County section (Site 14), the wildflowers are best in April and May, but can vary widely in quality from year to year. Use the suggestions here as a loose guide to locations. If you see an obscure county road that looks promising, take it. A map atlas like DeLorme's *Texas Atlas & Gazetteer* is helpful to have on such an excursion. Most of the places described are on private land, so be sure to stay on the right-of-way.

TX 29 can have a good showing of wildflowers along it in both directions from Llano. It's a busy road, but the flowers can make the hassle of dealing with traffic worth it. Be sure to check on FM 1431 starting in Kingsland. Follow it north to TX 29. A classic scenic spot is where the railroad crosses the highway. The railroad is not in use right now and is publicly owned, so you're free to walk down the track

Longhorn cattle and bluebonnets (Lupinus texensis), *Llano County*

Railroad tracks near Kingsland with bluebonnets (Lupinus texensis), *Llano County*

for photos. Some years bluebonnets and Indian paintbrush can cover the rusty tracks, making for great compositions. Other years yellow flowers will be abundant.

Take FM 1431 north from TX 29, also. It and nearby FM 261 can sometimes be lined with fields of flowers, especially bluebonnets and Indian paintbrush. Be sure to explore some of the side roads in this area for other possible sites.

TX 71 is also busy, but can sometimes have good flower cover southeast of Llano toward Austin. Check some of the county roads along it northwest of the FM 2233 turnoff to Kingland. Likewise, there are often flowers along TX 16 heading south toward Fredericksburg. Be sure to drive some of the quiet county roads that fork off TX 16, especially those near Oxford. FM 152 toward Castell can be a good place for flowers, too.

Directions: Llano is a small Hill Country town about 75 miles northwest of Austin. It has lodging and restaurants.

16. Colorado Bend State Park

Colorado Bend State Park is a relatively quiet park on the north side of the Hill Country. It is located on the Colorado River at the very upstream end of Lake Buchanan. The river here flows in a good-sized canyon as it enters the lake.

Gorman Falls, a beautiful spring-fed waterfall, pours over a travertine bluff and fosters the growth of lush ferns and mosses. It requires a 1.5-mile guided hike or 3-mile self-guided hike, a worthwhile effort. (For tour information and a map of the area visit the park Web site, www.tpwd.state.tx.us/spdest/findadest/parks /colorado_bend.) The best time to shoot it consistently is on a cloudy day. Spring usually is the rainiest time of year, so it generally offers the best flow rates plus green vegetation. Summer

Gorman Falls, backlit. Colorado Bend State Park

can still be good, but the hike will be hot. If it's a sunny day, consider hiking to it in late afternoon when the waterfall goes into shadow. The image will have a cool bluish look, but can be corrected by adjusting your camera white balance to open shade, or fixed later in Photoshop. Sometimes good shots can be taken on sunny days early in the morning or with hazy sunlight to soften the contrast. Be sure to stay on the trail. The ferns and travertine formations can be easily trampled. Take a range of wide-angle to medium telephoto lenses.

Spring-fed Spicewood Creek flows into multiple pools and over cascades along the Spicewood Springs Trail. Like Gorman Falls, it's probably best shot on cloudy days in the spring. Late afternoon can sometimes be good

The Eastern Hill Country 45

Inks Lake State Park wildflowers: bluebonnets (Lupinus texensis), *Indian blanket* (Gaillardia pulchella), *and bitterweed* (Helenium amarum)

if you arrive at the creek a little before the sun leaves the canyon bottom. A large pool at the start of the trail often attracts swimmers. Continue up the trail to more pools and cascades. A wide to normal lens works best.

With good light and skies, other shots include upland areas of the park at sunrise or sunset. On calm mornings or evenings, the sunrise and sunset sky can be reflected in the lake. If you're into cave photography, the park offers guided cave tours (advance reservations recommended; call 325-628-3240). These tours are not for the timid, with crawling, sliding, and climbing required. Take a waterproof, padded case for your camera and flash equipment, and prepare to get muddy and wet.

Directions: Colorado Bend is about 25 miles west of Lampasas near the village of Bend. Food and lodging are available in Lampasas and Llano. The park has a campground.

17. Inks Lake State Park

Inks Lake is a small, constant-level lake on the Colorado River downstream from Lake Buchanan. Much of the lakeshore of the park is developed, with campgrounds and picnic areas; however, a good sunset sky can be easily captured with lake reflections at many places along the shore. Inks Lake lies in the Llano Uplift area of the Hill Country. Pink Valley Spring gneiss outcrops everywhere and creates fertile soil favorable for wildflowers in the spring. Bluebonnets and Indian paintbrush are common in early April; many other flowers come up later. Blooming prickly pear cacti are plentiful. The flowers are best along the main park road, especially on the south side of the park, but be sure to explore some of the hiking trails as well. Try for compositions with flowers in the foreground and the lake in the background.

On chilly, still mornings from late fall to early spring, mist will sometimes form over the water, offering great side- and backlit photos as the golden light of the rising sun hits it. Be in position at dawn. One of the best spots to catch the first light and mist is at the point just north of the park store and boat ramp.

Another good photo spot is at Devil's Waterhole in the northeast part of the park, beyond campsite 246. (A downloadable map is available at the park Web site, www.tpwd.state .tx.us/spdest/findadest/parks/inks.) A tributary flows into the lake here in a narrow, rocky channel with pools and cascades. Above it is an overlook that offers a good location from which

to shoot at both sunrise and sunset. Access the overlook via Park Road 4 rather than by climbing up to it from Devil's Waterhole.

Directions: Inks Lake is off Park Road 4, south of TX 29 between Burnet and Llano. The park offers many campsites. Both Llano and Burnet have plenty of motels and restaurants.

18. Longhorn Cavern State Park

The tunnels and chambers of Longhorn Cavern wind around under the wooded hills that rise to the east of the Colorado River Valley and Lake LBJ. The cave has few decora-

Longhorn Cavern, Longhorn Cavern State Park

tions such as stalactites and stalagmites, but its smoothly sculpted limestone walls have their own appeal. The Civilian Conservation Corps dug a large amount of mud out of the cave and built the trails in the 1930s.

For the best shooting in the cave, you need a tripod. Because tripods are not allowed on regular guided tours, call ahead (877-441-2283) and set up a photography tour. You can take pictures on a regular tour, but your time is more limited so you'll need to work fast to get shots. (See Caverns of Sonora, Site 5, for cave photography tips.) Although there aren't many formations, your guide will probably point out some nice calcite crystals that are worthy of close-up shots.

Some of the most interesting and easiest shots are in the cavern entrance. Natural bridges above and the CCC-built stone steps of the trail make good subjects. The old stone CCC buildings and structures on the surface make good subjects after your tour.

Directions: Longhorn Cavern is on Park Road 4 to the west of US 281, between Marble Falls and Burnet. Both towns offer many restaurants and motels. Nearby Inks Lake State Park has a large campground.

19. Enchanted Rock State Natural Area

The huge granite dome that rises out of the hills north of Fredericksburg offers some of the best photography in Central Texas. It's an exposed mass of a large billion-year-old granite batholith. Enchanted Rock is a good location for photos all year, although it's hot in summer. Plan to hike to the summit of the main dome for sunrise or sunset. A few lone trees growing in cracks in the rock, pools left by recent rainfall, and the scattered boulders on the slopes all offer good potential for photos. A great sky

Boulders on main granite dome at dusk in Enchanted Rock State Natural Area

just adds to the mix when it happens. Carry a small headlamp for the hike down. You'll want to stay up on top until the last light fades.

Once you've spent time shooting on the main dome, consider climbing some of the smaller rocks: Freshman Mountain, Little Rock, Buzzard's Roost, and Turkey Peak. (Visit the park Web site for maps of the area: www.tpwd.state.tx.us/spdest/findadest/parks /enchanted_rock.) The first two probably offer the most variety. Like the main dome, sunrise and sunset are best. Bring everything from very-wide-angle lenses to telephotos. You'll find a use for every lens.

When you're up high on the rocks, consider getting people into your photos for scale. Action shots of subjects hiking, running, and jumping are particularly good. For rock-climbing photos, the best place is on the sheer north face of Enchanted Rock late in the day. If you have the skills, consider rappelling down to or climbing up to the climbers for vertigo-inducing wide-angle shots of them on cliff faces high above the ground. For closer, more intimate climbing photos, hike into the big boulder area on the marked climber trails on the west side of the main dome above Echo Canyon.

Consider walking to Moss Lake for reflections of Enchanted Rock at sunset. In wet springs, the fertile granitic soils at the base of the rocks usually offer good wildflowers. Enchanted Rock is worthy of multiple visits. Different seasons, weather, and light offer something new every trip.

Directions: Enchanted Rocks is on FM 965 north of Fredericksburg. The park offers a walk-in tent campground. Fredericksburg has a large selection of restaurants and lodging choices.

A vernal pool on the main granite dome, Enchanted Rock State Natural Area

Willow City Loop winter scene

20. Willow City Loop

The Willow City Loop is one of the most popular wildflower drives in Texas from mid-March to mid-May. The igneous soils in the area seem to be made for bluebonnets. The hills and fields along parts of the drive can be completely blanketed with the blue lupine in good years. That's the good news. The bad news is that the route has become extremely busy during wildflower season. If at all possible, avoid the drive on weekends.

One of the nice things about the drive is that most of it is not fenced, making compositions easier than on many Texas roads. However, you must stay on the right-of-way. The landowners along the route have gotten irritated in recent years with hordes of trespassing visitors trampling their flowers and fields. Because of that, sheriff deputies patrol it regularly during peak season. Signs caution against stopping or parking, but unless you stray from the road, this is generally not enforced.

Sam Ealy Johnson cabin, LBJ National Historical Park, Johnson Settlement

The drive can be started at either end. Drive north from Fredericksburg on TX 16 to FM 1323 on the right. Follow it about 3 miles east to the hamlet of Willow City. Turn left onto Willow City Loop. The road soon reaches the scenic part, a viewpoint overlooking a valley below and some sizable hills rising above. In a good year the valley below will be covered with bluebonnets. Slow down and watch carefully as you descend into the valley. Bluebonnets will become more common. Stop and shoot when you see a composition that appeals. Some large live oaks along the road add to the area's beauty.

In about 3 miles the road turns west into a surprisingly deep canyon, probably the most scenic part of the drive. Blooming yuccas here often add variety to the bluebonnets carpeting the ground. After the road climbs out of the canyon to the west, the terrain flattens out, but the flowers can still be good all the way to TX 16. White prickly poppies are often mixed in with the bluebonnets here. Both sunny and cloudy days work for the flowers. When it's cloudy, shoot narrower, closer compositions that don't include much sky.

Directions: The Willow City Loop is just northeast of Fredericksburg, as described above. Fredericksburg has many restaurants and motels.

21. LBJ State Park and National Historical Park

The state park and part of the national park lie along US 290 about halfway between Freder - icksburg and Johnson City, by Stonewall. Johnson City hosts the other part of the na- tional park. Both sections have features worth photographing, especially if you like old build- ings and farm scenes.

LBJ State Park and Historic Site, Sauer-Beckmann Farmstead

The Sauer-Beckmann Living History Farm at the Stonewall section offers the rustic buildings of a farm from the early 1900s, complete with staff dressed in period costume engaged in farm chores. You can photograph livestock, the old barn (don't miss the interior; bring a tripod), the garden, and the staff making soap, tilling the garden, rendering lard, and doing a multitude of other activities. A very small dose of fill flash will help light faces if you photograph the park staff.

The historic Danz cabins lie on the west side of the Stonewall section. They can be very attractive with early or late light. Some years they can be surrounded by bluebonnets, Indian paintbrush, and other flowers in April and May.

The drive along RR 1 offers good views of the Pedernales River, especially at sunrise and sunset. Try framing the river with some of the trees on the bank, or wait for reflections of the sunrise or sunset sky to appear on a still day. Drive east a short distance on RR 1 to get to the bridge that crosses to the north side of the park. The bridge offers good river views with the right light. Just across the river are the Junction School and the reconstructed LBJ birthplace home. Both may be worth a shot or two in the right light. The classic Trinity Lutheran Church along RR 1 looks great late in the day.

The well-marked Johnson City section of the park is just southwest of downtown. There are several historic buildings worth photographing here, especially early and late in the day. The Johnson cabin, the Bruckner Barn, and the Polk Johnson barn are probably the most interesting. The grounds can have good bluebonnet coverage in April. Tight shots of bluebonnets next to the old split-rail fence that surrounds the park are particularly nice.

Don't miss taking a few shots of the old Johnson City courthouse on the other side of US 290 from the park. The limestone building is an architectural jewel worthy of both wide-angle shots and telephoto detail shots. If you have one, bring a tilt-shift lens. As usual, you'll have the best light for photos early and late in the day. During the Christmas holidays, the courthouse and the Pedernales Electric Coop buildings near the LBJ Visitor Center are spectacularly decorated with Christmas lights. The best shooting is at dusk while there's still a little light in the sky. Don't miss it. The nearby town of Blanco also has a beautiful historic courthouse.

Directions: The two sections of the park are in Johnson City and along US 290, as described above. Both Johnson City and Fredericksburg have plenty of restaurants and lodging choices.

22. Old Highway 9

The old route from Fredericksburg to Comfort is a scenic back road worthy of photographing. It follows the route of the old railroad that once connected Fredericksburg to the Guadalupe River Valley. If you look closely along the drive, you can sometimes spot the old railroad grade, especially near the middle of the route.

The route is best done early or late in the day when the shadows are long and the light more rich. Drive slowly and look for rural shots—horses in the field, winding road views, old stone buildings. From Fredericksburg, drive east past the edge of town on US 290 to Old San Antonio Road on the right, marked with "Old Tunnel Wildlife Management Area" signs. Follow the road south all the way to FM 473 near Comfort.

The road slowly climbs up to the divide that separates the Pedernales and Guadalupe river valleys. Initially the road crosses more open, rural country. Then the terrain gets increasingly hilly. At the divide the railroad went through a long tunnel. Brazilian free-tailed bats have taken up residence in the abandoned tunnel. The state purchased the property, the Old Tunnel Wildlife Management Area, and offers tours and talks. Up to three million bats live in the tunnel from May to October. The bats fly out at sunset, so be sure to get there a little early if you want to photograph them. Normal to wide lenses generally work best. Afterwards, grab a great burger at nearby Alamo Springs Cafe.

South of the tunnel, the road drops into the narrow valley of Block Creek. The first bit of sunrise light and the last bit of sunset light are blocked here. However, some of the hills are good subjects in early light. Depending on water levels, Block Creek can look attractive at the crossing. Old Highway 9 ends at FM 473, but don't stop yet. Continue straight toward Comfort. At sunrise, there are some good views across fields of the rising sun on the left. For a really nice view of the Guadalupe River, turn left onto FM 473 at the junction. In a short distance turn right on the county road to Waring. Drive a short distance to the river crossing. Cypresses line the river here, making for good shots, especially upstream. If you continue on a bit farther, you'll hit the village of Waring. There's an old-fashioned gas station in the middle of town that's worth a few shots.

Directions: Get to Old Highway 9 from Fredericksburg as described above. From Comfort, take FM 473 about 5 or 6 miles east to the

On a county road to Waring: bald cypress trees along the misty Guadalupe River in first light

junction right before FM 473 turns right and crosses Block Creek. Both Fredericksburg and Comfort have plentiful restaurants and lodging.

23. Cave Without a Name

If you like caves, you'll love Cave Without a Name. Although the cave has been open for tours for years, it is much less well known than Caverns of Sonora or Natural Bridge Caverns. However, it's very scenic and worthy of photographing. It has multiple chambers, a flowing stream, and plentiful decorations such as stalactites, stalagmites, and columns.

The best time to shoot during regular tours of the cave is when the guide stops to talk about cavern features. (See Caverns of Sonora, Site 5, for cave photography tips.) You'll get the best shots if you call ahead and set up a photography tour (830-537-4212). You can use a tripod on these tours, useful given the dim light (tripods are not allowed on regular tours), and you'll have more time and flexibility to set up shots.

Directions: From Business US 87 (Main Street) in Boerne, go east on FM 474 for about 7 miles. Turn right on Kreutzberg Road and follow it about 4 miles to the cave gate on the right. Drive to the parking area. Boerne has plentiful lodging and restaurants.

24. Cibolo Creek

Cibolo Creek is a small part of the Boerne City Park on the east side of Boerne that's great for an afternoon of shooting. It's part of the town's complex of parkland that includes everything from ball fields to the Cibolo Nature Center. The nature center has a restored marsh, natural prairie, and the permanent flowing waters of Cibolo Creek. When you arrive, pick up a trail map at the Nature Center to guide you to the best areas for photography.

Cibolo Creek, along the south side of the

Cave Without a Name

park, is most photogenic. The eastern section of the creek probably has the best photo spots, with sizable bald cypress trees lining the creek. Cloudy days are best for photographs, enabling you to avoid the high-contrast light that results with sunshine when shooting along the creek. On sunny days, come late in the day for the last golden rays of sun. When the sun slants down toward the horizon, the tall grasses of the prairie make for a nice subject, along with the ponds of the restored marsh.

Directions: From the center of Boerne at the junction of Main Street/US 87 Business and TX 46, drive east along TX 46 to City Park Road on the right (south side). Turn right on City Park Road and follow it a short distance past the ball fields to the Nature Center entrance on the right. The park is open daily from 8 am to dusk.

25. Guadalupe River State Park

The Guadalupe River drains a large section of the central Hill Country, rising to the west of Kerrville and flowing east through New Braunfels. It's worth photographing along much of its length, but lies largely on private land. That makes the state park one of the best places to shoot the river. In the park, the river has cut a narrow valley through the juniper-and-oak-covered hills. The best photos are found along

Cibolo Creek, near Boerne

Bald cypress trees on the Guadalupe River

Guadalupe River with rainbow, Guadalupe River State Park

the river itself. Flat stretches of clear water alternate with gentle rapids. Towering bald cypress trees rise from twisted roots on the water's edge. Soft overcast light is easiest for this type of shooting; however, the river on the east side of the park catches early morning light, offering opportunities for sunny shots. Be there at dawn, though. The light quickly gets too harsh.

Normally, the light between mid-morning and mid-afternoon isn't the best for photos. However, the clear river water picks up a nice green-blue look under strong light and clear blue skies. A polarizing filter will often cut the water's reflections and glare from green foliage, adding richer color to the shot. Just be careful not to let any sky in the composition get unnaturally dark.

April is the best month to photograph here, when the trees have bright, spring-green foliage. Summer is good as well, although the trees and vegetation will be a darker green. In November, the cypress trees sometimes turn a rusty orange. On cold winter mornings, mist over the river can create moody views. The park is busy in summer and on weekends in spring and fall.

Directions: The park lies along TX 46 between Boerne and the TX 46/US 281 junction in Spring Branch. It has a good campground. Food and lodging are plentiful in Boerne.

26. Honey Creek State Natural Area

Honey Creek State Natural Area adjoins and is managed by Guadalupe River State Park. The creek is a beautiful jewel, a permanent stream that winds down through a canyon to the Guadalupe River. Unlike the dry upland areas, the creek is lined with bald cypress, sycamore, pecan, cedar elm, and other trees. Columbine, maidenhair fern, and palmetto thrive along the rocky creek banks. Endless close-up and medium views are possible.

To protect the delicate vegetation, the natural area has very limited access. Two miles of trails wind through the area, open only to guided tours. As of this writing, tours are scheduled every Saturday morning at 9 am. Call the park (830-438-2656) to confirm tour dates and times. Although a guided tour is not the ideal way to get photos, the area is beautiful and worthy of the trip. If possible schedule

Honey Creek, Honey Creek State Natural Area

your trip for a cloudy day. It's best to shoot here with soft light. The bright greens of spring make that time of year the ideal time to visit.

Directions: The natural area adjoins Guadalupe River State Park, which lies along TX 46 between Boerne and the TX 46/US 281 junction in Spring Branch. The state park has a good campground. Food and lodging are plentiful in Boerne.

Soda-straw stalactites, Natural Bridge Caverns

27. Natural Bridge Caverns

Natural Bridge Caverns is one of the most extensive caves in Texas. It has large chambers and beautiful natural formations. It's also conveniently located just a few miles off I-35 between San Antonio and New Braunfels.

The cavern is relatively well lit, but still dim by photographic standards. If tripods are allowed on your tour, take one. (See Caverns of Sonora, Site 5, for cave photography tips.) Highlights include the natural bridge at the cavern entrance, Sherwood Forest, Castle of the White Giants, and the Hall of the Mountain King. All feature large formations, particularly massive stalagmites.

Although the regular tours will allow you to take decent photos, for the best possible images, get together with some like-minded individuals and arrange for a group tour emphasizing photography. You'll pay more than for the regular tour, but it will be worth it. Call a week or more ahead (210-651-6101) to schedule. Consider taking a bright flashlight or portable spotlight to brighten up dark areas while on a photography tour.

Directions: Go northwest on Natural Bridge Caverns Road/FM 3009 for 8 miles into the Hill Country from Exit 175 on I-35 north of San Antonio. Both New Braunfels and San Antonio have a multitude of dining and lodging choices.

28. Gruene and the Guadalupe River

Gruene was a small German settlement on the Guadalupe River that's now part of New Braunfels. The nature and landscape photographer will like the river, just upstream of the bridge. Take the road down to the river from the small historic business district. The river here flows through some rapids and under the

Gruene Mansion Inn at dusk

bridge. On summer weekends you'll probably have to park in the big lots on the east side of the business district and walk the short distance down to the bridge. As is the case with most of the river, the land on its banks is private, so if you want to walk upstream, you'll have to wade in the river. Bring water shoes and wade carefully—rocks are slick and there are deep holes. There are attractive rapids and cypresses here to shoot. In summer, especially on weekends, you'll be able to photograph kayakers, tube riders, and boaters as they float by.

There are several historic buildings in town that are photogenic, particularly the Gruene Mansion Inn. Gruene Hall, next door, built in 1878, is the oldest continuously running dance hall in Texas. Many famous musicians have played here over the years. For photos it often looks best at dusk. After you're done shooting, you can pay the entrance fee and relax to some live music.

River Road follows the Guadalupe upstream from Gruene to the large dam that creates Canyon Lake. There are many scenic spots to shoot along the way, but most of them lie on private land, and parking is tight. The best way to shoot this stretch of river is to rent a raft or canoe, pack your camera gear in a waterproof case that is secured to your boat, and spend a day paddling and shooting. There are

Historic Gruene Hall with Christmas lights at dusk

a few moderately difficult rapids that you may wish to portage rather than risk your gear by paddling through them. Floating the river is big business here, so come on weekdays if you can, ideally in spring or fall.

Directions: Gruene is just off TX 306 on the north side of New Braunfels. Take Hunter Road south from TX 306 a short distance into the center of Gruene. There is lodging and dining in Gruene and nearby New Braunfels.

29. San Marcos River

The San Marcos River starts flowing abruptly at a huge group of springs that gush out of the Edwards Aquifer in the small city of San Marcos. The springs are contained within a small dammed lake managed by Texas State University just off Aquarena Springs Drive. Drive through the golf course and park at the cluster of buildings at the lakeshore. Fish, turtles, and water plants are clearly visible in the crystal clear water. Glass-bottomed boats allow you to float out onto the lake and look down at the springs below.

Wander along the lakeshore and boardwalk for close-up and medium views of the lake and shoreline. Use a long telephoto to capture images of waterfowl, turtles, and other wildlife. Spring and summer, when the vegetation is green, is probably the best time of year for photography. Sunrise or cloudy days offer the best light. The water is a constant 68 degrees, so on chilly mornings, mist can often form over the lake and river downstream. The mist gives photos a moody look, while obscuring distant

Spring Lake, source of the San Marcos River, in the morning mist

clutter. Water flows over the small dam in two places. The eastern spillway is the most attractive for photos when shot from below the dam. Below the dam, the river winds through university and city parks, offering plentiful close-up and medium views. The river is popular with tubers, kayakers, and canoeists, allowing for photos of water sports, especially in summer. The best spot for kayaking shots is at a low dam made to appear natural that stirs up some great whitewater. It lies just upstream of the Cheatham Street bridge at Rio Vista Park.

Directions: San Marcos lies on I-35 between Austin and San Antonio. Lodging and restaurants are plentiful.

30. Wimberley

Wimberley is a quaint, tourist-oriented town tucked into the hills northwest of San Marcos. The Blanco River is a pretty, cypress-lined river that flows through the town. Unfortunately, there is very little public access to the river. River Road, which turns left from RR 12 just west of the main square, follows a beautiful stretch of the waterway, but parking and ingress to the river is almost nonexistent. However, there are a few places that photographers can reach that are very worthwhile.

Park at the square downtown and walk onto the bridge just west of the square for nice views of Cypress Creek. The spring-fed stream is

Kayaking the whitewater in the San Marcos River

Cypress Creek, Wimberley

lined with cypress trees, and looks good from spring through fall. If you cross to the far side of the bridge, you can drop down the bank to the creek on the south side of the bridge. For an even nicer access point, walk across the square to where a street angles into the square on the northeast side by some shops. Walk a few feet up the road to a small park and playground on the left. A trail leads out of the back side of the park down into the creek's floodplain. The trail follows the creek upstream for maybe a half mile, offering multiple views of the creek, with its pools, cascades, and cypress trees. Soft light is best. Be sure not to cross the creek; the other bank is privately owned.

After walking along Cypress Creek, go back to the street facing the park. Drive about a half mile east along the road, away from the square. Just past a large cemetery, turn left onto another street and drive a short distance between the cemetery and a currently unoccupied church building to the entrance to Blue Hole Park. Blue Hole is an area of deep swimming holes along Cypress Creek, a short distance upstream from the walking trail. Large cypresses and clear, blue-green water make for great photos, especially on cloudy days. In summer it is a popular place for swimming, so come early in the morning if you don't want people in your shots. In fall the cypresses turn rusty orange. As of 2011, the park was undergoing a lot of development, so access hours may be irregular for some time.

For a different type of photo, drive west on

Blanco River, Wimberley, at sunrise

RR 32 from its junction with RR 12 on the south side of Wimberley. In a few miles, you will come to a narrow ridge high above the Blanco River Valley known as the Devil's Backbone. The best views are from along the road just east of the picnic area. Late afternoon and sunset offer the best light for photographs.

Directions: Wimberley is a small town about 15 miles northwest of San Marcos on RR 12. It has both food and lodging.

31. Krause Springs

Krause Springs is a beautiful oasis tucked into the hills near Lake Travis. The 115-acre property has been in the Krause family for more than 50 years. Thirty-two springs surface here. By far the main attraction is the high bluff over which the flow of several of the springs cascades. The water has deposited travertine covered with lush maidenhair ferns. The water tumbles into a sizable pool that is popular with

Krause Springs waterfall with cypress trees

swimmers in summer. Large cypresses around and downstream from the pool also make good photo subjects.

Generally the best time to shoot here is in the spring right after the vegetation leafs out. Summer is also good, but come early if you don't want swimmers in your shots. Cloudy days tend to work best, but late in the day when the sunlight is diffused by haze can also be good for photography.

Directions: Take TX 71 about 30 miles west of Austin (about 7 miles west of the Pedernales River Bridge). Turn right on Spur 191 by the Exxon gas station, go a short distance, and turn right again on County Road 404. The springs will be on your left. Krause Springs offers camping. Food and lodging is available in the Lake Travis area and in Austin.

32. Pedernales Falls State Park

The Pedernales River rushes over a series of limestone ledges and creates a number of cascades at Pedernales Falls State Park. Start your trip by driving to the end of the main park road. (Maps are available at park headquarters and online at www.tpwd.state.tx.us/spdest /findadest/parks/pedernales_falls.) Walk down to the falls area, a massive expanse of limestone that has been scoured clean of vegetation by numerous floods over the years. Explore the area for good compositions that include some of the small waterfalls and channels carved into the rock. Because the river flows east here, the best light tends to be at dawn, and shooting then ensures that there won't be people in your photo. Weekdays are much less busy than weekends at the popular park. Sunlight works better than cloudy light. Spring usually has the highest flow rates. Mist can rise over the falls on chilly mornings from late fall to early spring.

Pedernales Falls with morning mist, Pedernales Falls State Park

Pedernales River

at the falls, the park only allows you to view and photograph from a viewing platform above. This area is best during a rainy spring on a cloudy day.

If you like bird photography, the park has an elaborate blind that pulls in many species. Early or late in the day works best.

Directions: Pedernales Falls State Park lies along FM 3232 about 6 miles north of US 290 between Dripping Springs and Johnson City. The park has a large campground. Johnson City has both food and lodging.

33. Hamilton Pool and Reimers Ranch

Hamilton Pool was a huge underground cavern that collapsed long ago, leaving a large overhanging grotto that faces down a canyon. A stream flows over the rim and free-falls 50 feet into a large jade-green pool that is popular with swimmers in summer. A cloudy day in spring generally offers the best shooting conditions. The flow rate of the waterfall is most likely to be high then and the vegetation will be green. If you don't want people in your shots, come as soon as the park opens in the morning (9 am). Some of the best views are with a very-wide-angle lens from the trail in the back of the grotto. On very rare occasions during extended periods of below-freezing weather, large icicles can form on the grotto roof because of the waterfall and seeping water.

Be sure to hike down the canyon below the grotto to the Pedernales River. The trail passes some nice pools and small cascades, along with cypress trees. All are great for close-up to medium-view shots. As at the grotto, cloudy skies will serve you best here.

Nearby Milton Reimers Ranch Park, while not quite as impressive as Hamilton Pool, is worthy of a visit. It has a total of 2,427 acres in a mix of park and preserve land. It consists of

Although there is not much vegetation in the falls area, other parts of the river are treed. Drive to the picnic area and walk down to the river, where you'll find bald cypresses. They can be especially attractive in fall, when the needles turn rusty red. The best light here is probably about an hour after dawn or an hour before sunset.

Twin Falls is another good destination for photographers. Take the short trail that loops between sites 15 and 20 in the campground. To protect delicate ferns and other vegetation upland terrain, narrow canyons, and 3 miles of Pedernales River frontage. If you like outdoor sports photography, the park is noted for mountain biking trails, rock climbing, and fishing. The limestone cliffs above the river attract the climbers, plus contain some small grottos decorated with ferns. Several of the small canyons that flow into the river have cypresses, pools, and small cascades that are especially attractive during rainy periods. The grottos and

Hamilton Pool

canyons are best photographed on cloudy days, but some of the upland areas have large expanses of grassland with widely scattered oak trees that can be beautiful right before sunset. Also, late in the day, try for shots of the river, framing it with trees along its banks or from the bluffs above. The Pogue Springs Preserve part of the park is beautiful, with a narrow canyon and spring-fed stream, but it has access restrictions to protect its delicate vegetation. Inquire at the park office about access when you visit Reimers Ranch.

Directions: To get to Hamilton Pool, drive west of Austin on TX 71 through the town to Bee Cave. Turn left on FM 3238/Hamilton Pool Road and drive 13 miles to the entrance on the right. The entrance to Reimers Ranch is also on FM 3238, about a mile before the entrance to Hamilton Pool.

34. Westcave Preserve

The 75-acre park contains concentrated beauty that makes up for its small size. It's a short side canyon off the Pedernales River. Because of its depth and narrowness, sun and wind have far less drying power, resulting in a lush environment of ferns, mosses, and other plants thriving along the small stream in the bottom. Bald cypress trees tower overhead. At the back, the canyon ends abruptly in a moist

Grotto at Westcave Preserve

grotto with caves and a small 40-foot waterfall that trickles down off the canyon rim. Travertine formations deposited by running water hang down from the grotto ceiling.

Before the park became a preserve, it was badly trampled and damaged by trespassers and others. Today, the preserve offers access only through guided tours on weekends. However, it's easy to get good shots on the tours. Check the park Web site (www.westcave .org) for current tour times. Bring lenses from normal to as wide as you have, and a tripod for the dim light. A round-trip trail less than a mile long gives great access. A cloudy day in spring, when the vegetation greens up and rainfall is highest, is the best time to visit. Sunlight is too high-contrast in the narrow canyon. Don't let rain stop you: cover your camera with a plastic cover and wear rain gear. The lush, dripping vegetation will make you think you're photographing the rain forest.

Directions: Drive west of Austin on TX 71 just past Bee Cave. Turn left on FM 3238 /Hamilton Pool Road and drive 14.5 miles to the bridge over the Pedernales River. The preserve entrance is on the right just after you cross the river.

Crockett Garden Spring and Falls along Good Water Trail, Lake Georgetown

35. Lake Georgetown

Lake Georgetown was created when the Army Corps of Engineers dammed the North Fork of the San Gabriel River in 1979. Unlike most lakes in Texas, the Corps owns the land surrounding the lake, creating an undeveloped shoreline with extensive access and photo opportunities. Sunsets and sunrises are always great for lake shots, particularly when the sky is lit up with colorful clouds. In the morning when the lake is most likely to be still, you can get reflections of the sky in the water. Visitors Overlook near the dam headquarters, Jim Hogg Park, and Russell Park offer good sunset potential. Jim Hogg, Russell, and Cedar Breaks parks offer sunrise views.

The Good Water Trail loops around the entire lake. The 11 miles between Cedar Breaks and Tejas Parks on the more rugged south shore are the most scenic. The best section is probably the first 2.5 miles of the trail, heading west from Cedar Breaks Park. High, sheer bluffs along the first part of the route offer great lake and sunset views with a range of lenses. Carry a flashlight if you stay out until sunset.

View of Lake Georgetown from bluffs on the Good Water Trail

Crockett Garden lies about 2.5 miles down the trail. A large spring bubbles up out of the ground here, just outside the Corps of Engineers lake property boundary. It then flows across the trail and over a substantial waterfall. Over many years the mineralized water has deposited a large amount of overhanging travertine that is covered with ferns during the warmer months of the year. Take a wide-angle lens and a macro. Cloudy days work best to minimize contrast. Very late in the afternoon will also work because direct sunlight leaves the falls area. You'll need to warm up photos taken under those conditions to get rid of the blue cast of open shade photos.

Directions: Lake Georgetown is a short distance west of Georgetown, just south of FM 2338. The lake offers camping at the parks mentioned above. Georgetown has plentiful lodging and restaurant options.

36. Private Ranches

The vast majority of Texas is privately owned, and the Hill Country is no different. Not surprisingly, many private ranches have beautiful features. In recent years a number of ranches have opened their gates to nature photographers for a fee. Some are best for landscape photography. Others concentrate on wildlife and are equipped with blinds and feeders. Unlike on public lands, you won't be tripping over other visitors. Some ranches provide food, lodging, and guide services on-site. Advance reservations are necessary. Visit www.images forconservation.org/landownermembers for information about the ranches that cater to nature photographers.

Block Creek Natural Area (a private ranch) along old Highway 9

Texas State Capitol rotunda dome

III. Austin

Austin is a large, booming city on the eastern edge of the Hill Country. It straddles the Balcones Fault, the huge fault that allowed the Hill Country to rise up to the west as a plateau. The city offers photographers everything from a modern skyline filled with skyscrapers to historic buildings to hidden natural areas. The University of Texas and state government still dominate much of the central city.

37. Texas State Capitol

The Italian Renaissance Revival–style capitol building dominates the north end of downtown. The 308-foot-tall building, sheathed in pink granite quarried from the Hill Country near Marble Falls, is one of the most beautiful buildings in Texas. It was built between 1882 and 1888 and paid for by trading over three million acres of public land in the Panhandle to the builders. The land became the XIT Ranch, the largest in the world at the time.

The photo possibilities here are endless. Late afternoon and early morning are probably best for photographs, along with dusk, when the lights come up. The south side of the building is probably the favorite of photographers. Try framing the building with the large trees and various monuments on the capitol grounds. A tilt-shift lens is useful to help correct perspective problems. Use wide-angle

Texas State Capitol

The Austin skyline is reflected in Lady Bird Lake.

lenses for broad views of the building. Tele-photos are good for shooting architectural details. Stormy skies can add drama to your photos.

Don't neglect the inside of the building. Take shots from the bottom of the rotunda of the dome high overhead. Shoot the ornate House and Senate chambers. Photograph details. Everything in the building was custom-made for the capitol, from the door hinges to the light fixtures. Use a tripod for the interior shots.

The Governor's Mansion is across 11th Street from the capitol. As of 2011, the beautiful building is being restored after a major ar-

son fire. When completed, the views from the fence on Colorado Street will capture the building nicely, especially early in the morning.

Directions: The Texas State Capitol is on the north side of downtown at the head of Congress Avenue. There is on-street meter parking, as well as public parking garages on the east side of the capitol along San Jacinto Street.

38. Downtown Skyline

For the classic view of Austin's skyline, cross the First Street Bridge over Lady Bird Lake to the south shore. Walk along the shoreline trail for many views of the skyline. Areas just west of the bridge (Auditorium Shores) and just east of the bridge offer some of the best views. When the lake is still, the skyline reflects in the lake. Late afternoon usually gives the best light. Stay through sunset. Occasionally clouds in the sky will light up over the city as the sun sets. At dusk, the sky dims and lights become visible in the buildings. Walk across Riverside Drive to the Long Center for the Performing Arts and the Palmer Events Center. Both building complexes offer interesting architectural details and alternative views of the city skyline.

Another spot for views is the big footbridge over the lake just east of the Lamar Boulevard Bridge. Afternoon through dusk is the best time there, too. If you're hungry, grab a bite at Joe's Crab Shack, at 600 E. Riverside, and while there get some nice views of the skyline across the lake from the restaurant's deck. This spot works both late in the day and early in the morning. Another more distant, but nice late-day and evening spot is the pavilion on the lake's hike and bike trail at the mouth of Barton Creek.

Directions: At Auditorium Shores by the First Street Bridge, there is a parking lot on the west side of the southern bridge approach and also some street parking on Riverside Drive. Both are often full late in the day, the best time for photographs, so allow time to find a parking spot. There is parking at the west end of Riverside Drive just after it crosses Lamar Boulevard by the Zachary Scott Theatre. Like at Auditorium Shores, parking can be difficult late in the day. Joe's Crab Shack is on the shoreline along Riverside Drive a few blocks east of Congress Avenue. For the final location, drive west along Barton Springs Road. Turn right into Zilker Park just after crossing the bridge over Barton Creek. Park along the park's drive where it makes a sharp left curve to the west. Walk down to the pavilion on the trail on the lakeshore below.

39. Downtown

Downtown Austin offers photography potential for architecture, nightlife, live music, and people. Interesting historic buildings can be found along 6th Street. The highlight is the Driskill Hotel. It will be difficult to avoid parked cars and traffic in your photos, but the best views are from across the street. 6th Street is known for its bar scene, so hang out on a

Frost Bank building at dusk

Historic Driskill Hotel in dusk light

and modern skyscrapers such as the Frost Bank Tower and the Austonian. A number of historic mansions, now mostly law offices, lie north of 6th Street along San Antonio, Rio Grande, and Nueces Streets and West Avenue.

Generally early and late in the day is best for photography, but the shadows and contrasts created by the buildings allow great shooting any time of day. Shoot through dusk as the lights come up and even into the night. If you're into shooting live music, inquire at the many downtown clubs and music venues for permission. Many lie along 6th Street east of Congress and in the Warehouse District.

Directions: Downtown is in the center of the city. Parking is a problem. Be patient and you'll eventually find a curbside spot or a public parking garage. Be prepared to walk a lot to find good locations.

40. Lady Bird Lake

Lady Bird Lake is in the center of Austin, created by a dam on the Colorado River. Much of the lakeshore is parkland. A hike and bike trail loops around much of the lake. The lake offers many nice photo viewpoints of the downtown skyline as discussed in the downtown skyline section (see Site 38). It also offers good shots of woodsy trails and, in the spring, blooming redbud trees on the north shore. For outdoor sports shots, it's hard to beat. Rain or shine, you can almost always find runners, walkers, and cyclists on the trail. The best time to shoot here is early or late in the day in spring.

One of the most scenic sections of the lake is on the south shore, where Barton Creek flows into the lake. The trail here jogs a short distance up Barton Creek (it's a small arm of the lake) and crosses the creek on an attractive footbridge before returning to the main lakeshore. The trail here is particularly well lined with woodlands. The footbridge makes a

Friday or Saturday night for interesting shots. Halloween and Mardi Gras are particularly entertaining.

The Warehouse District, centered around 4th and Guadalupe Streets, offers more nightlife and interesting older buildings. Congress Avenue, the main street through downtown anchored by the Capitol at the north end, has an interesting mix of ornate old buildings good viewpoint for shooting views of the creek, the main lake, and the distant buildings of downtown.

The lake is a popular site for water sports. Canoes and kayaks are in abundance here, particularly at Barton Creek. In addition, rowing teams practice on the lake. The shoreline trail offers good views of the boats. The footbridges just east of the Lamar Boulevard Bridge and underneath the Loop 1 (Mo-Pac) freeway bridge give interesting, sometimes abstract views of the boats from above. Rent a canoe at Barton Springs (just up the creek from the Barton Creek foot bridge) for different views of boaters, the skyline, and the lake.

For architectural shots, don't miss the Long Center for the Performing Arts and the Palmer Events Center, both on the south shore of the lake just west of South First Street.

In summer, a million or more bats live in the crevices under the Congress Avenue Bridge over the lake. Get there a half hour before sunset and hope the unpredictable bats will make their massive evening exodus before dark. Shoot from either the hike and bike trail under the bridge on the south shore or from the bridge itself.

Directions: To shoot the Barton Creek area of the lake, go to Zilker Park. It lies along Barton Springs Road west of Lamar. Turn right into

Long Center for the Performing Arts

Zilker Park Oriental Garden

Zilker just after crossing the road bridge over Barton Creek and find a spot along the park road. For the Loop 1 (Mo-Pac) footbridge over the lake, turn onto Stratford Drive from Barton Springs Road in the middle of Zilker Park. Follow it a short distance to the bridges of Loop 1. Park on the right in the gravel lot under the bridges. Park in the Austin American-Statesman parking lot on the east side of the Congress Avenue Bridge on the south shore after business hours to view the bats.

41. Zilker Botanical Garden

The Zilker gardens are a beautiful attraction in Zilker Park and a great spot for garden photos. Winter can be drab, but the rest of the year, especially spring, pops with color. The 30-acre grounds have numerous photo opportunities. Highlights include the Japanese Garden, with its arched wooden bridge, ponds, and miniature waterfalls, and the Rose Garden, with its white gazebo. In early spring, the small Azalea Garden can be beautiful. The relatively new Hartman Prehistoric Garden features beautiful pools, walks, and a great dinosaur sculpture. Several old buildings in Pioneer Settlement can make interesting photo subjects.

Because of heavy tree cover, be sure to come on a cloudy, still day rather than a sunny day. Generally normal to wide lenses will be most useful, along with a macro for flower close-ups. A moderate telephoto will occasionally be useful for isolating details.

Directions: The entrance to the botanical gardens is on Barton Springs Road in the center of Zilker Park between Lamar Boulevard and Loop 1 (Mo-Pac).

42. Barton Creek

Barton Creek is a large seasonal drainage that starts west of Austin in the Hill Country and joins Lady Bird Lake at Zilker Park. It cuts a substantial canyon through the rocky hills, with high cliffs and a crystal clear creek that flows part of the year. Within the city, the creek lies within the Barton Creek Greenbelt and is lined with hiking and mountain-biking trails. It offers a nice creek, lush woodland, hiking, biking, and rock climbing. Generally early in the morning, late in the afternoon, and cloudy weather offer the best times for photos. It's most beautiful when the creek is running, most likely in spring and early summer.

Rock climbers tend to favor the cliffs between the Spyglass and Loop 360 access points. You definitely want a cloudy day to photograph climbers. Two small waterfalls up-

Barton Creek cascades, Barton Creek Greenbelt

A hiker on the Barton Creek Greenbelt

stream from the Loop 1 (Mo-Pac) entrance offer great photo opportunities with normal to wide lenses. Twin Falls in particular is popular with swimmers. It's about 0.5 mile upstream from Loop 1. Sculpture Falls is more photogenic, but requires another mile or so of hiking upstream. On warm days with good water flow, get there early if you don't want people in your shots. Weekdays are better than weekends. The water is sometimes flowing at Sculpture Falls even if it's dry at Twin Falls. If you want to shoot a popular, beautiful, partially developed swimming hole fed by natural springs, be sure to go to Barton Springs at the northern terminus of the Greenbelt.

Directions: The Greenbelt is in close-in southwest Austin. The lowest access point is in Zilker Park (on Barton Springs Road west of Lamar) right by Barton Springs. The Spyglass access point is on Spyglass Drive, reached from the northbound frontage road of Loop 1 (Mo-Pac) between Loop 360 and Bee Caves Road. The Gus Fruh access point is on Barton Hills Drive in the Barton Hills neighborhood, accessed by taking Barton Skyway north from South Lamar Boulevard and turning left on Barton Hills Drive. The Loop 360 access point is on the northeast side of Loop 360 a little north of Lamar by a big office building in the creek valley bottom. Don't park in the office building parking lot; you might be towed. The Loop 1 access point is by the big Loop 1 bridge over Barton Creek on its frontage road just south of Loop 1's intersection with Loop 360.

43. University of Texas

The University of Texas sprawls across many acres north of the state capitol complex. The

University of Texas Tower and Littlefield Fountain

campus has a number of attractive buildings, some old, some modern, that lend themselves to architectural photography. Most of the more attractive older buildings are centered around the prominent UT Tower, the tall building on the west side of campus. Try both wide-angle views framed by live oak trees using tilt-shift lenses if you have them and tight views of architectural details. The Blanton Museum of Art on the south side of campus along MLK Boulevard offers interesting shots both inside and out.

A classic view is of the Tower rising up behind the Littlefield Fountain on 21st Street. Try shooting in late afternoon or dusk, when the lights come on. Another nice view is of the Tower in the distance above the more modern-style fountain on the East Mall, just west of San Jacinto Street. This view works best early in the morning or at dusk. There is another attractive fountain on the grounds of the LBJ school on the east side of campus on Robert Dedman Drive. The fountain makes a good foreground for shots of the interesting LBJ Library building or the distant Tower. Mid-afternoon sun to dusk works best for shooting here.

Directions: The university lies just north of the capitol complex. Parking can be a challenge. If possible try for evening hours and during Christmas and spring breaks or the

Michener Gallery building, second-floor mezzanine, Blanton Museum of Art

Mayfield Park peacock

breaks between summer sessions. There are public parking garages toward the north end of San Jacinto Street, the north end of Speedway across from the Petroleum and Chemical Engineering Building, along Martin L. King just west of San Jacinto, and just west of campus at San Antonio and 25th Streets.

44. Laguna Gloria and Mayfield Park

These two sites are located in a beautiful older section of the city near Lake Austin. Laguna Gloria is an art museum on the grounds of the estate of Clara Driscoll on the east shore of Lake Austin. The landscaped grounds hold the Italianate-style home of Driscoll, now used as an art exhibition space by the Austin Mu-seum of Art. Many views of the attractive home are possible using the gardens, trees, and a fountain as compositional elements. Sculpture decorates some of the grounds. A walking trail loops out onto a wooded peninsula that juts into Lake Austin. It offers nice woodsy scenes and views of the lake. Depending on what you're shooting, both sunny mornings and afternoons and cloudy days will work for photos here.

Pretty Mayfield Park, adjoining Laguna Gloria on W. 35th Street, was donated to Austin in 1971 by Mary Mayfield Gutsch. It has 2 acres of gardens and 21 acres of woodland with walking trails. The water-lily-covered ponds and colorful peacocks that wander the grounds are probably the most attractive photo features. Try wide-angle to normal lenses for the ponds or use a telephoto to zoom in on a peacock, possibly with one of the ponds in the foreground. Generally soft light works best in this location. Spring, with its fresh green vegetation, is the best season to photograph here.

Directions: Laguna Gloria and Mayfield Park are at the west end of W. 35th Street. Exit onto 35th Street from Loop 1 (Mo-Pac) and go west to its end near the shore of Lake Austin.

45. Mount Bonnell

The popular high hill of Mount Bonnell overlooks the west side of the city and Lake Austin. It rises steeply from the shore of Lake Austin immediately to its west and from beautiful older residential neighborhoods on its east. The best views lie to the west of the lake and West Lake Hills beyond. Late afternoon sun is essential for good photos here. Walk north from the pavilion on the summit for some of the best views of Lake Austin. With a wide-angle lens you can get some of the rocky ledges of the hill in the foreground with the lake and other hills in the distance. Take a friend to pose in the shot for scale. Stay until the sunset light fades from the sky.

Directions: From Loop 1 (Mo-Pac) exit on 35th Street and go west, toward Lake Austin. Near the end of 35th, turn right on Mount Bonnell Road. Cross a small bridge and climb steeply up a big hill to the parking lot on the left at the summit.

46. Loop 360 Bridge

The Loop 360 Bridge (Pennybacker Bridge) was completed in 1982 to carry the highway across Lake Austin. The bridge was built as a huge steel arch to eliminate the need for center supports that would be a boating hazard on busy Lake Austin. Built into a high bluff on the

Overlooking Lake Austin from Mt. Bonnell

The Loop 360 (Pennybacker) Bridge

north side, the bridge is an attractive structure worthy of photos. To get the best view, drive to the north side of the bridge and get in the southbound lanes of Loop 360. Park on the right side of the road just before the big road cut that leads to the bridge. Be very careful of the fast-moving, heavy traffic here. A well-worn path leads to the top of the hill above the road cut. Several viewpoints atop the cliffs give great views of the bridge, the lake, and the city beyond. Late afternoon sunshine offers the best light for these shots. Be careful on the cliff edges. Alternately, drive to the south side of the bridge and park at the boat ramp at the base of the bridge. You can get views looking up at the bridge from here. The bridge is dark-colored and not well lit, but dusk shots with car headlights and distant city lights are possible as well.

Directions: Drive on Loop 360 to the bridge where it crosses Lake Austin.

47. McKinney Falls State Park

McKinney Falls State Park lies on the southeast side of Austin. It's a popular 744-acre park with hiking and bike trails, camping, and picnicking. It's centered around the confluence of Onion and Williamson Creeks. In the park,

Onion Creek drops over two large limestone ledges, creating two small waterfalls. Both are photogenic, but especially Lower Falls. It has a higher ledge with numerous water channels carved into it and more water because of Williamson Creek's contribution. Both falls are best photographed at first light. Cloudy days also work. The Rock Shelter Interpretive Trail that starts by the Smith Visitor Center also has photo possibilities, including a large rock shelter (best on cloudy days) and views of Onion Creek. Spring after the vegetation has turned green is the best time of year to photograph here. Winter can occasionally have moody mist at the falls on cold mornings.

Directions: The easiest way to get to the park is to drive east on TX 71/Ben White Boulevard to US 183. Go right, south, on US 183 to McKinney Falls Parkway on the right. Follow the parkway a few miles to the park entrance on the right.

Onion Creek, Lower Falls, McKinney Falls State Park

The Alamo at dusk

IV. San Antonio

The large city of San Antonio straddles the southeastern edge of the Hill Country. The Spaniards first founded a mission there in 1718, giving the city a long, rich history. The old missions, the River Walk, and other attractions draw many photographers to the city.

48. The Alamo

Everyone in Texas needs a photo of the Alamo. The old building, once a Spanish mission church, is famous as the site of a major battle between Mexican and Texan troops during the Texas War of Independence.

It's difficult to get creative images of the famous facade of the main building, as the site draws numerous tourists. Consider visiting during a cold winter day if you don't want people in your shot. The building faces west, so late afternoon is the best time for good light, although late in the day the light is blocked by downtown buildings to the west. The Alamo photographs well at dusk, too, when the lights come on and the sky fades to a deep indigo. If you like dusk shots and don't want people in the frame, consider coming about an hour before sunrise. After you get your classic Alamo

Walkway, Alamo

San Antonio's River Walk

shot, wander around the grounds and shoot the courtyard, walkways, old live oaks, and anything else that catches your eye. Be sure to check out the beautiful lobby of the historic Menger Hotel on the plaza.

Directions: The Alamo is on the east side of downtown near the River Walk, at Alamo and Houston Streets. Expect to pay for parking, either in a garage or surface lot.

49. The River Walk

As with the Alamo, no visit to San Antonio is complete without a few shots of the River Walk. Unlike at the Alamo, it's easy to get a good variety of photos here. Stroll along the sidewalks on the riverbank and look for compositions. The river lies below street level, so be sure to climb up on some of the bridges, such as the ones at Commerce and Market Streets, for views down onto the River Walk. If you have a tilt-shift lens, use it to correct perspective. Wide-angle lenses are most useful, but bring a few moderately long lenses for isolating details. Unlike most places, midday with a good blue sky is a good time to photograph here if you pick the bright and dark areas of your photos carefully. Cloudy days even out the light, but don't include much sky in your photos. Bring a tripod and hang out until after sunset. Get some shots after the city lights have come on and the sky still has a bit of lingering

The River Walk at dusk

blue. Spring and summer yield perhaps the best shots because the plants are green. During the holiday season, Christmas lights decorate many of the big cypress trees, adding extra color to dusk and night shots. Use caution when using a tripod in the area, as the sidewalks can be crowded with pedestrians.

The River Walk has recently been enlarged. You can photograph all along it, but the older central section has most of the colorful sidewalk restaurants and shops, so concentrate your time there.

Directions: The River Walk is downtown, centered around Commerce and Market Streets. Parking can be a hassle; expect to pay for parking in a garage or lot.

50. Southwest School of Art

The Southwest School of Art occupies a beautiful complex of buildings that was once the Ursuline Convent founded in 1851. A museum and tours tell more about its history. The old limestone buildings have a French Gothic style that offers many architectural photo opportunities. Large oaks soften the buildings and add color. Be sure not to miss the interior of the chapel, a beautiful structure with stained-glass windows. In general, cloudy days are probably best for photographs here. Wide-angle and tilt-shift lenses will be needed most.

Directions: The school is on the north side of downtown at 300 Augusta Street, adjoining the River Walk.

Chapel exterior and courtyard, Southwest School of Art

Central Library building, San Antonio

51. Central Library

While visiting the Southwest School of Art (Site 50), cross Augusta Street and walk over to the Central Library a block away on Soledad Street for a different style of architecture. It's a large, six-story, modernist-style building painted reddish-orange with highlights of other bright colors. Its stark design, repeating patterns, colorful details, and landscaped courtyards offer lots of interesting views for the architectural photographer. Late afternoon brings golden light and attractive patterns of light and shadow. Early morning can also be a good time to shoot here. Wide-angle lenses are essential. Tilt-shift lenses and moderate telephotos for details would also be useful.

Directions: The library is at 600 Soledad St., on the north side of downtown, about a block from the River Walk.

52. San Fernando Cathedral

San Fernando Cathedral is a beautiful old church in the middle of downtown. It's tucked in with other buildings, so you have to crop fairly tightly to not get adjoining clutter in your shot. You can get good detail shots with a moderate telephoto in addition to the entire front facade with wider lenses. The ornate front is

San Fernando Cathedral interior

sunlit in the morning, but you can't get first light because other buildings block it. Partial views of the white limestone front work in the afternoon even though it's in shadow, provided you don't put much sky in the composition. Don't neglect the interior. Take as wide a lens as you have. As always, tilt-shift lenses help correct perspective with architectural shots. Be respectful. If a church service is going when you arrive, wait until it ends before photographing. The old Spanish Governor's Palace lies only a half block away, as does the reddish stone Bexar County Courthouse. Both also make interesting photo subjects.

Directions: The cathedral is in the heart of downtown on Commerce Street right near the intersection with Flores Street. Parking can be difficult. Be patient and look for a public parking garage or lot.

53. King William Historic District

Prominent Germans settled the area in the 1800s, creating the most elegant residential district in the city at the time. The 25-block area on the east bank of the San Antonio River is still one of the most beautiful neighborhoods

Guenther House, King William Historic District

in the city. Substantial historic homes with immaculate grounds line the quiet streets. Sunny days from early to mid-morning and mid- to late afternoon are the best times for architectural photo fans to shoot here. Most are private homes, so be respectful and shoot from the sidewalks and streets, rather than trespassing into yards.

Directions: The district lies south of downtown, south of E. Durango Boulevard roughly between S. St. Mary's Street and the river.

54. McNay Art Museum

The McNay is a premier art museum, worthy of a visit regardless of whether you take photos. The main building is a beautiful stucco structure with a red-tiled roof; the extensive landscaped grounds offer many views of it. One of the nicest views is from the large fountain in front. The inside courtyard is also attractive. A wide-angle lens is necessary. The interior also offers great photo opportunities. To protect the artwork, no tripods or flashes

McNay Art Museum

San Antonio Botanical Gardens Conservatory

are allowed inside. Photos cannot be taken of exhibitions with art that the museum does not own. Commercial use of photos requires a permit from the museum. Generally, late afternoon and cloudy days work best for the exterior. The grounds are most beautiful in spring. While you're there shooting, be sure to tour the galleries. You're an artist, right? Enjoy some world-class art while you're visiting.

Directions: The museum is about 5 miles north of downtown near the junction of New Braunfels Avenue and Austin Highway, at 6000 N. New Braunfels.

55. San Antonio Botanical Garden

You can easily spend an entire day shooting in the 33-acre gardens. Whether it's sunny or cloudy, you'll find something worthy of capturing. Some of the most interesting areas for photos are the formal gardens near the entrance, the Japanese Garden, and Fountain Plaza. Late in

Ruiz House, Witte Museum

the day, the landscaped hill with the overlook is attractive, as is the pond and old cabin in the East Texas Pineywoods section of the gardens. A highlight is the large glass conservatory. Its geometric shapes combined with lush plant life make for interesting photos both inside and out. Take a full range of lenses. Sooner or later you'll want them all. Don't forget a macro for flower close-ups. Take a small folding reflector to shade sun off close-up views of flowers or to reflect light where needed. A tripod is also helpful for macro shots.

Directions: The garden lies several miles north of downtown, at the intersection of N. New Braufels Avenue and Funston Place.

56. Brackenridge Park

Large Brackenridge Park is San Antonio's premier city park and has many attractions worthy of photos. The Japanese Tea Garden at the northwestern side of the park offers great shots, especially in spring and summer. Cloudy light usually works best here. The San Antonio River flows through the park, offering a nice water feature. Early and late in the day give the best light for shooting the river and much of the rest of the park grounds. The Witte Museum has interesting old buildings and sculptures on its grounds. The extensive San Antonio Zoo is here, offering the opportunity to shoot exotic species in settings that appear relatively natural. Bring a long telephoto for the zoo, both to zoom in on animals and, with a wide aperture, to blur out busy backgrounds. Plan to spend at least a half day at the zoo.

Directions: The park lies several miles north of downtown between Broadway and US 281 at 3700 N. St. Mary's St.

57. San Antonio Missions National Historical Park

No photo trip to San Antonio would be complete without getting some images of the old Spanish missions. Beginning in 1718 the Spaniards founded a chain of five missions along the San Antonio River. The first is now known as the Alamo (see Site 48). The other four are managed by the National Park Service and the Catholic Church. The largest and most impressive is Mission San José, with its massive church and large surrounding courtyard. Try for photos of the church with a telephoto from farther away and close-ups with a wide angle. Frame the church using doorways and the ruined convent arches. Use a tripod for interior shots both here and at the other mis-

Mission Concepción framed by mesquite tree

Mission Concepción at dusk

sions. Don't miss the old restored mill. This mission is the most popular, so it's difficult to get broad shots without people. Come on weekdays in winter for the smallest crowds. Stay until the park closes the courtyard to get the best possible light on the church. Sunny days are best.

Mission Concepción is also a large church, but with much smaller grounds. Be sure to shoot the original ceiling frescos in the convent. Because the church faces west, you'll have the best light for photographing the structure late in the day. Try to frame the church with some of the trees on the grounds and use a variety of lenses and distances to shoot it. Generally, wide-angle and tilt-shift lenses work best here.

Mission San Juan is much smaller, but offers nice interior shots and good views of the church and grounds at sunrise. Try framing the church with some of the ruined walls that surround it. Except for sunset silhouettes of the bell tower, late afternoon light generally won't give you great results here.

Mission Espada is on the south edge of San Antonio and has a nice rural feel. Like at San Juan, most of the historic buildings except for the church are in ruins. The old stone church facade is very interesting, with a broken arch around the doorway, old wooden doors, and the bell tower above. Be sure to come for sunrise when the light is best. Like Mission San Juan, evenings don't work as well, unless there is a good sunset to silhouette the bell tower against. The nearby stone Espada Aqueduct, still in use, is worthy of a shot or two on a cloudy day.

Directions: All four missions are south of downtown, along the San Antonio River. Directions are complicated. The National Park Service (www.nps.gov) has a good map online.

Mission Concepción's arched walkway

Sunrise Locations

Fort McKavett State Historic Site
San Antonio Missions, Mission San Juan
San Antonio Missions, Mission Espada
Highway RM 337
Enchanted Rock State Natural Area
Pedernales Falls State Park
South Llano River State Park, Llano River

Sunset Locations

Fort McKavett State Historic Site
Austin, Downtown Skyline
Austin, Texas State Capitol
Austin, Loop 360 Bridge
San Antonio Missions, Mission Concepción
Enchanted Rock State Natural Area

Austin skyline at dusk

Hikes

Westcave Preserve grotto

A climber on the Prok route, Enchanted Rock State Natural Area

Springs along Devils River

Views

Enchanted Rock State Natural Area
Hill Country State Natural Area,
   Twin Peaks Trail
Highway RM 337

Water

Amistad National Recreation Area,
   Pecos River Arm
Devils River State Natural Area
Austin, Lady Bird Lake
Honey Creek State Natural Area
Colorado Bend State Park, Gorman Falls
West Cave Preserve
Hamilton Pool